The Africa News Cookbook
African Cooking for Western Kitchens

The Africa News Cookbook
African Cooking for
Western Kitchens

Edited by Tami Hultman
Designed and illustrated
by Patricia Ford

Africa News Service, Inc.
Publisher
Durham, North Carolina

Africa's cuisine is as little known as its politics, its economies or its art. Yet where there are limited ingredients, African cooks have developed imaginative variations for otherwise monotonous diets. And where there is abundance, they have created culinary masterpieces.

This book is dedicated to a wider appreciation for the food of Africa and to the hope that freedom from hunger—that most basic of human rights—will one day belong to all the people of that vast and lovely continent.

Published in the United States of America in 1985
Africa News Service
Box 3851, Durham, North Carolina 27702
919-286-0747

Library of Congress Catalog Card Number
84-73540

ISBN 0-9614368-0-8

732-3481

All of us at Africa News Service were a part of the production of *The Africa News Cookbook*.

Editorial Board: Reed Kramer, president; Charles Ebel, managing editor; Charles Cobb; Lise Ebel; Tami Hultman; Seth Kitange; Jim Lee; William Minter; Katharine Somerville.
Associate Staff: Susan Anderson, Mills Crosland, Pat Ford, Deborah Jackson-Ricketts, Ruth Minter, Debbie Nickell, Robin Surratt, Sharon Whitmore.**Intern:** Rob Peterson

Project Coordinator for Africa News Service: Julie Wynne

Index: Susan Anderson

Typesetting by Liberated Types, Ltd., Durham, North Carolina

Paste-up: David Southern, Bull City Studios, Durham, North Carolina, with help from Deborah Jackson-Ricketts and Patricia Ford

Color separation (cover): Color Graphics, High Point, North Carolina

Printed by Neuberg Photography and Printing, Hayfork, California, a member shop of the Graphics Communications International Union

References

In preparing *The Africa News Cookbook,* we consulted every collection of African recipes we could find. As far as we could discover, only two were in print or available in North America at our press time:

> *Good Tastes in Africa*
> The African and Africa-Related Women's Association of the University of Illinois at Urbana-Champaign
> Compiled by Rebecca Dyasi
> Edited by Louise Crane

To order, send a check for $6.00, made out to the University of Illinois, to the African Studies Program, University of Illinois at Urbana-Champaign, 1208 West California, Room 101, Urbana, Illinois 61801.

> *Tanti Ama's African Cookbook*
> by Zinta Konrad, Amet Binder Akyea, and Ofosu Akyea. Dzika Publications, Madison,WI.

To order, send a check for $4.95 plus .80 for postage and handling, made out to Tanti Ama, to 3200 Trappers Cove, Apt. 2C, Lansing, MI 48910. The book is a collection of west African recipes.

Other sources we consulted, some of which are in the collections of larger libraries, include:

The American Women's Association of Rabat. *Cooking in Morocco.* (no date).

Ayensu, Dinah Ameley. *The Art of West African Cooking.* New York: Doubleday and Company, 1972.

Bayley, Monica. *Black Africa Cookbook.* San Francisco: Determined Productions, Inc., 1971.

Biarnès, Monique. *La Cuisine* Sénégalaise. Dakar: Societé Africaine d'Edition.

Coetzee, Renata. *Funa-Food from Africa.* Durban, South Africa: Butterworth and Co., 1982.

Cook with Nigeria (a recipe collection printed in Lagos).

Cornucopia Project of Rodale Press. *Empty Breadbasket? The Coming Challenge to America's Food Supply and What We Can do About It.* Emmaus, PA: Cornucopia Project, 1981.

De Almeida Chantre, Lourdes Ribeiro. *Cozinha de Cabo Verde.* Bolama: Imprensa Nacional de Cabo Verde, 1979.

Dede, Alice. *Ghanaian Favourite Dishes.* Accra, Ghana: Anowuo Educational Publications, 1969.

Hachten, Harva. *Kitchen Safari.* New York: Atheneum, 1970.

Lesberg, Sandy. *The Art of African Cooking.* New York: Dell Publishing Co., Inc., 1971.

Mars, J.A. and Tooley, E.M. *The Kudeti Book of Yoruba Cookery.* Lagos: C.M.S. (Nigeria) Bookshops, 1959.

Mendes, Helen. *The African Heritage Cookbook.* New York: MacMillan, 1971.

Moten, Bea. *200 Years of Black Cookery.* Indianapolis: Leonbea.

Odaatey, Bli. *A Safari of African Cooking.* Detroit: Broadside Press, 1971.

Ominde, Mary. *African Cookery Book.* Nairobi: Heineman Press, 1975

Parry, John W. *Spices.* New York: Chemical Publishing Company, 1969.

Parry, John W. *The Spice Handbook.* Brooklyn: Chemical Publishing Company, 1945.

Purseglove, J.W. *Spices.* London: Longman, 1981.

Robertson, Laurel; Flinders, Carol; and Godfrey, Bronwen. *Laurel's Kitchen.* Berkeley, CA: Nilgiri Press, 1976

Rombauer, Irma S. and Becker, Marion Rombauer. *Joy of Cooking.* Indianapolis, IN: The Bobbs-Merrill Company, Inc., 1975.

Sandler, Bea. *The African Cookbook.* New York: World Publishing, 1970.

Timitimi, A. O., *Ijo Cookery Book.* Ibadan, Nigeria: University of Ibadan, 1970.

van der Post, Laurens, and the Editors of Time-Life Books. *African Cooking.* Foods of the World. New York: Time-Life Books, 1970.

Wilson, Ellen Gibson. *A West African Cookbook.* New York: M. Evans and Company, Inc., 1971.

Wolfert, Paula. *Couscous and Other Good Food from Morocco.* New York: Harper and Row Publishers, 1973.

Acknowledgements

Recipes in this book are from many people and places. In the editing and testing process, all have been adapted so that we could present a consistent style and approach. (If you shared a favorite recipe with us, but you do not recognize it here, that's probably why.).

Recipes on the following pages have been adapted from or were enriched by information from: *Cooking in Morocco*—10, 22, 28, 38, 39, 61, 62, 63, 74, 113, 114, 121, 128, 136, 139, 143, 148, 155; *Cozina de Cabo Verde*—14, 84, 85, 89, 149; *Ethiopian American Cookbook*—2, 26, 27; *Funa*—29; *La Cuisine Sénégalaise*—43, 90, 91; *Indian Delights*—45, 46, 47, 48, 52, 140; "The Bridge" magazine (winter, 1976;'77)—93; "Barbara Baëta's West African Favorites Cookery Cards" (Accra, 1972)—101; "Blue Band Vegetarian Recipe Cards" (Nairobi)—104, 109, 129; the Nyala Restaurant, New York, NY—110; The African-American Institute, School Services Division—148, 153.

Recipes on the following pages have been adapted, with the kind permission of the authors, from: *Kitchen Safari*— 71, 80, 109, 114, 117, 147; *The Art of African Cooking*— 73, 113, 84, 85, 89, 92, 139, 146, 148; *Good Tastes in Africa*—76 (Farida Cassimjee), 107 (Margaret Fivawo), 112 (Emily Bavu), 115 (Emily Bavu), 116 (Lorraine Crummey), 153 (Rebecca Dyasi), 154 (Rebecca Dyasi).

Recipes on the following pages are reprinted from: *Good Tastes in Africa*—3 (Lorraine Crummey); *The Spice Handbook*—5,6; *Cooking in Morocco*—54.

Many people contributed to the cookbook by advising us, by submitting their own versions of African dishes, and by testing and tasting the recipes we gathered. In a few cases, recipes arrived by mail without return addresses. Our thanks to those anonymous friends and to:

Suzette Abbott, Ahmad Abd-Shakur, Sadiyah Abd-Shakur, Madjid Abduallah, Leigh Adam, Mel Adam, Peter Adkins, Dwight Agner, Embassy of the Democratic and Popular Republic of Algeria, Cathy Alguire, Ray Almeida, Daniele Armaleo, Winifred Armstrong, Andy Barco, Dan Barco, Susan Barco, Timmy Barco, W. D. Beukes, Lisa Blumenthal, Sallie Brown, Ann Brunger, Scott Brunger, Burkina Faso Mission to the United Nations, Tom Campbell, Embassy of Cape Verde, Bessie Corrington, Fatou Kiné Ciss, Maris Corbin, Louise Crane, Claudia DiBona, Erin Echols, Hettie Ellis, Jimmy Ellis, Valariano Ferrão, Aden Field, Laurie Fox, Aurelia Franklin, John Hope Franklin, Julie Frederikse, Susan Gerbeth-Jones, Carol Gilly, Larry Gilly, Arthur Gordon, Rivka Gordon, Dub Gulley, Fadzai Gwaradzimba, Jim Harb, Richard Harkrader, Ki Henderson, Doug Henderson-James, Nancy Henderson-James, Russell Herman, Pam Jaskot, Sheridan Johns, Richard Johnson, Elmo Kitange, Neema Kitange, Sia Kitange, Kwin Hultman Kramer, Roban Hultman Kramer, Bruce Landon, Derin Laughter, Tris Laughter, Malik Lee, D. Livingstone, Doris Marshall, Judith Marshall, John Mayfield, Thomas Carter Mayfield, Cathy Murphy, Kakona Nekongo, Javier Nelson, Anne Newman, Assia Nour, Mac O'Barr, Pat Palmer, Jake Phelps, Mark Pinksy, Unette Pistorius, Helene Pruniaux, Scott Ricketts, Rich Robeson, Esme McClinton-Rose, Vernon Rose, Embassy of the Republic of Rwanda, Steve Schewel, Rama Seck, Karen Shelley, Karen Sirker, Embassy of South Africa, Bisi Sowunmi, Olumide Sowunmi, Segun Sowunmi, Stephanie Spottswood, Curt Stager, Atieno Stanford-Asiyo, Embassy of the Democratic Republic of Sudan, Cathy Surles, Jeff Sykes, Embassy of the Republic of Uganda, John Valentine, Trip Van Noppen, Ken Vickery, Desire Volkwijn, Kay-Robert Volkwijn, Lynne-Corinne Volkwijn, Helen Whiting, William Whitmore, Peter Wood.

Special thanks for special efforts to:

Ron Bunch
Lonna Harkrader
John Havran
Jean Hultman

Anne Lippert
Elmira Nazombe
Peaches Rigsbee
Stephanie Urdang

The publication of this book was made possible by Mac Jernigan, Wellspring Grocery and Esther Wynne.

Contents

Preface

Far from his southern home on a wintry day in New York, a young black man is drawn to a street vendor by the smell of yams cooking:

> I stopped as though struck by a shot, deeply inhaling, remembering, my mind surging back, back. At home we'd baked them in the hot coals of the fireplace, had carried them cold to school for lunch...Yes, and we'd loved them candied, or baked in a cobbler, deep-fat fried in a pocket of dough, or roasted with pork and glazed with the well-browned fat; had chewed them raw—yams and years ago.

The narrator of Ralph Ellison's novel, *Invisible Man*, buys one yam and returns for two more. "I yam what I am," he explains to the man at the coals. "Where I come from we really go for yams." Both the play on words and the evocative nature of the yam itself are testimonies to the rich meanings of African foods in North America.

Like sesame, cumin, peanuts, okra and rice, yams were brought to colonial America from Africa, where they can be as culturally significant as they were for Ellison. In fact, the word *yam* itself is derived from the verb *to eat* in several west African languages—as in the Fulani *nyami*.

It is appropriate that an African recipe book be produced in the southern United States, a region that long ago assimilated African ingredients and culinary techniques. Every "southern" cookbook silently exhibits its debt to those heartstick slaves who re-created a bit of home in their stews and cornbreads and greens and fritters. African influences are pervasive, from the jambalayas and gumbos of Louisiana bayous to Charleston's characteristic bene snacks—peppery, sesame crackers and sesame candies and cakes. Indeed *gumbo*, or *gombo*, is the word for okra in such west African languages as Wolof, Mandingo and Bambara, while *bene*, or *benne* means *sesame* in Umbundu and Tshiluba, languages of Angola, Zaire and Zambia. Even our word *banana*, though the tree itself is of Asian origin, comes from Africa by way of Portugal with spelling intact.

Wider acknowledgement of those roots is overdue, as is the acquaintance of North Americans with the foods represented here.

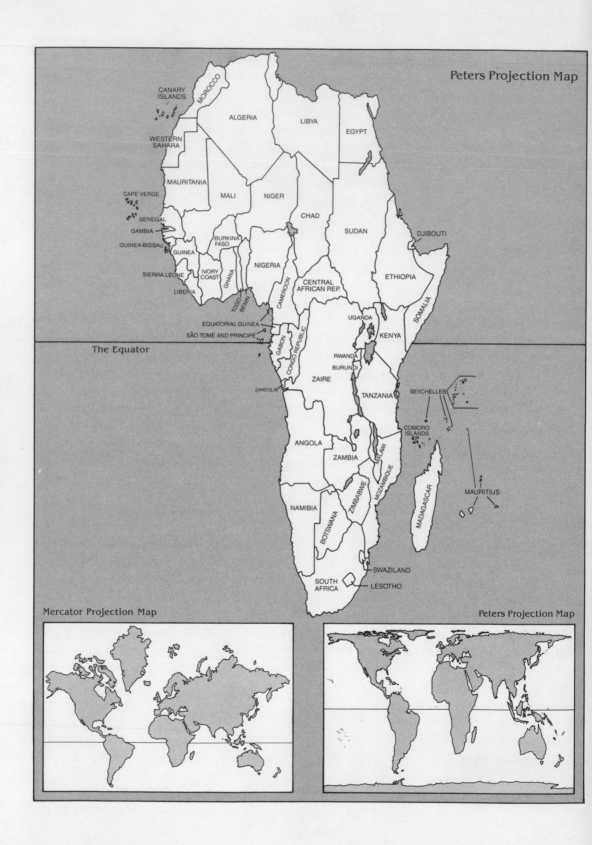

Peters Projection Map

CANARY
ISLANDS

MOROCCO

ALGERIA

LIBYA

EGYPT

WESTERN
SAHARA

MAURITANIA

MALI

NIGER

CHAD

SUDAN

DJIBOUTI

CAPE VERDE

SENEGAL

GAMBIA

GUINEA-BISSAU

GUINEA

BURKINA
FASO

NIGERIA

ETHIOPIA

SIERRA LEONE

IVORY
COAST

GHANA

LIBERIA

CENTRAL
AFRICAN REP.

TOGO

BENIN

CAMEROON

EQUATORIAL GUINEA

SÃO TOME AND PRINCIPE

UGANDA

SOMALIA

KENYA

The Equator

GABON

CONGO REPUBLIC

RWANDA

BURUNDI

(ANGOLA)

ZAIRE

TANZANIA

SEYCHELLES

COMORO
ISLANDS

ANGOLA

ZAMBIA

MALAWI

NAMIBIA

ZIMBABWE

MOZAMBIQUE

MADAGASCAR

MAURITIUS

BOTSWANA

SWAZILAND

SOUTH
AFRICA

LESOTHO

Mercator Projection Map

Peters Projection Map

Introduction

Our World—Not What We Thought

We grew up with the Mercator projection map. It has been so much a part of our world view for four centuries that anything different seems heretical, almost as absurd as claiming the earth is flat. And yet, Mercator-based maps significantly distort the relative sizes of the globe's land masses. Europe's four million square miles appear as large as Africa's 11.7 million. North America's 11 per cent share of the earth's surface looks significantly larger than Africa's 16 per cent.

The Peters projection, developed by West German historian Arno Peters, is an attempt to equalize the distortions inherent in any flat map, and so to present a more realistic picture of our world. By startling us, and shaking our sense of what we assume to be true, the Peters map may be one step towards modifying many of our misperceptions about Africa.

The African continent is larger and more diverse than most of us have realized. Its climates range from arid to tropical, its topography from desert to grassland to dense rain forest to snow-covered mountains. Its people live in 54 nations and speak 2,000 languages and dialects. In parts of Ethiopia or Burundi, they are likely to be over six feet in height, while in areas of central Africa or Namibia, anyone reaching five feet would be considered tall.

Culture and cuisine are equally varied. And there are, in Africa as in most of the world outside North America, vast differences between cities and villages, between the lifestyle of urban and rural peoples. Also, as elsewhere, scientific and technological developments as well as the erosion of traditional social systems mean constantly changing work and eating patterns.

But two common generalizations are so broadly true as to be, forgivable. One is that the peoples of Africa are friendly and hospitable. Their generosity takes many forms, but it is a rare traveler to Africa who does not return with tales of being made welcome. In even the most modest home, that hospitality includes the lavish sharing of food.

The second truism is that Africa is the poorest continent. A complex interaction of many factors, including the worst drought in a century, means that 24 African countries face widespread starvation during the 1980's. Amid such scarcity, food becomes an international political issue.

The African Diet

Little is known about pre-colonial eating habits in Africa, but accounts by travelers and explorers suggest that in most of the continent, diets were more nutritious and food more plentiful than is the case today. Writings about southern Africa from the 16th and 17th centuries describe a people whose diet was based on milk and legumes, supplemented by meat from cattle or wild game, and numerous vegetables, fruits and grains. Commonly mentioned in early European accounts from around the continent are sesame, rice, corn, millet, beans, peas, squash, pumpkins, yams, okra, eggplant, spinach, onions, mushrooms, nuts, berries, mangoes, plums, dates, sugarcane and honey. In coastal areas, fishing rather than hunting or herding provided animal protein.

Of course, hunger was not unknown. Geared to self-sufficient subsistence, food production sometimes was inadequate when cultivation was hampered by drought, flood, conflict or other crisis.

Nevertheless, in much of the continent, the nutritive quality of the average diet appears to have declined. Only in the 1930's, for example, did maize, or corn, become a "staple" food of southern Africa, edging out the more nutritious millet that came to be known, disparagingly, as *kaffir corn*. In west Africa, earlier staples were similarly displaced by cassava, the starchy, low-nutrient import from Brazil.

And not until the colonial period did one-crop economies become normal, as agriculture was reoriented towards export production. In the process of becoming the supplier of half the world's cocoa, Ghana has produced less and less of its own food. Yet, if you find chocolate in Ghana today, it is almost certainly imported, since the processing that adds value to the cocoa bean is done elsewhere.

At the same time, more and more people have left farming altogether to work in mines and factories. As in the case of the switch from food to cash crop cultivation, the move towards wage labor sometimes resulted from marketplace incentives—the prospect of earning money in an increasingly monetized society. Too often the transition was coercive, whether through taxation, outright expropriation of land, or forced labor.

African Women and Food

Since the beginning of the United Nations Decade for Women in 1975, awareness about the role of women in the economies of poor countries has grown, although their contributions still are routinely overlooked. In Africa, women account for an estimated 80 per cent of agricultural labor, and in some countries they grow virtually all the food. Where men have moved to cities in search of work, rural women have been left unaided to carry water, fetch firewood, clear land, sow, weed and harvest crops, and preserve and process both wild and cultivated edibles. These tasks alone can take 15 hours a day. Then there are children and homes that need attention.

It is hardly surprising that among the most successful development projects are those that meet women's needs for clean, accessible water, replenishable sources of fuel, and labor and energy-saving devices such as oil presses and improved stoves.

A Hungry Continent

The causes of current African poverty are passionately debated in scholarly journals, international forums and in the media. Hunger in the 20th century has been attributed to many causes: the colonial legacy; the scars of the slave trade; contemporary economic relations between a wealthy, industrialized northern hemisphere and a poor, commodity-producing south; a lack of education and "know-how"; discrimination against women; incompetent and corrupt governments; and, of course, to the weather, which may be influenced by such human interventions as the destruction of rain forests. But all observers agree that, whatever the reasons, there is a crisis.

We at Africa News believe that we can all be part of the solution, by informing ourselves and by joining with others to take action. One idea is to get access to a restaurant or community center and use the recipes in this book to prepare an African dinner to benefit famine victims. Those who buy tickets might become the nucleus of a group that can continue working locally on hunger issues.

Following is a partial list of U.S.-based groups active in the African nations worst hit by the "great drought." Compiled by INTERACTION (the American Council for Voluntary International Action), it is not comprehensive, but it does include organizations that concentrate on development and self-help projects as well as those providing emergency relief. If you want to help, they are a good place to start.

Adventist Development and Relief Agency—6840 Eastern Avenue, NW, Washington D.C. 20012 (202) 722-6770

African Inland Mission—135 West Crooked Hill Road, Pearl River, NY 10965.

American Friends Service Committee—1501 Cherry St., Philadelphia, PA 19102 (215) 241-7000

American Jewish Joint Distribution Committee—60 East 42nd St. NY, NY 10165 (212) 687-6200

Africare—1601 Connecticut Ave., NW, Suite 600, Washington, D.C. 20009 (202) 462-3614

Baptist World Aid—1628 16th St., NW, Washington, D.C. 20009

CARE, Inc. - 660 First Ave., NY, NY 10016 (212) 686-3110

Catholic Relief Services—USCC—1011 First Ave., NY, NY 10022 (212) 838-4700

Christian Children's Fund—PO Box 26511, Richmond, VA 23261

Christian Reformed World Missions—2850 Kalamazoo Ave., SE, Grand Rapids, MI 49560

Church World Service—475 Riverside Drive, NY, NY 10115-0050 (800) 223-1310

continued on next page

Direct Relief International—Box 30820, Santa Barbara, CA 93130-0820 (805) 687-3694

Grassroots International— Box 312, Cambridge, MA 02139 (617) 497-9180

Heifer Project International—PO Box 808, Little Rock, ARK 72203

Interchurch Medical Assistance—Box 429, New Windsor, MD 21776 (301) 635-6474

Lutheran World Relief—360 Park Ave., South, NY, NY 10010 (212) 532-6350

MAP International—Box 50, Wheaton, IL 60187 (800) 225-8550

Mennonite Central Committee—21 South 12 St., Akron, PA 17501 (717) 859-1151

Oxfam America—Africa Crisis, 115 Broadway, Boston, MA 02116 (800) 225-5800

Presiding Bishops Fund for World Relief, The Episcopal Church—815 2nd Ave, NY, NY 10017 (212) 867-8400 Ext. 384

Salvation Army, World Service Office—1025 Vermont Ave, NW, Washington D.C. 20005

Save the Children Federation—Box 925, Westport, CT 06881 (800) 243-7075

United Church Board for World Ministries—475 Riverside Drive, NY, NY 10115

U.S. Committee for UNICEF—Box 3040, Grand Central Station, NY, NY 10163 (800) 826-1100

World Concern Development Organization—19303 Freemont Ave., N., Seattle, WA 98133 (800) 426-7010

World Neighbors—5116 North Portland Ave. Oklahoma City, OK 73112

World Relief Corporation—PO Box WRC, Weaton, IL 60187 (800) 535-LIFE

World Vision Relief Organization—919 West Huntingdon Drive, Monrovia, CA 91016 (800) 423-4200

YMCA, International Division—101 North Lacker Drive, Chicago, IL 60606

YWCA, World Relations Unit—135 West 50th Street, NY, NY 10020

For further information about any of the groups, contact INTERACTION at 200 Park Avenue South, New York, New York 10003 (212)777-8210.

The **Canadian Council for International Cooperation** is a source for information about development-aid groups based in Canada. Available materials include a handbook of member agencies. CCIC's address is 450 Rideau Street, 3rd floor, Ottawa, ONT K1N 5Z4 (613) 236-4547.

The following organizations can provide additional information about world hunger, including literature lists and suggestions for organizing local activities around food policy issues.

Bread For the World—802 Rhode Island Avenue N.E., Washington D.C. 20018 (202)269-0200

The Hunger Project—Box 789, San Francisco, CA 94101 (415) 346-6100

Institute for Food and Development Policy—1885 Mission Street, San Francisco, CA 94103-3584 (415) 648-6090

Rodale Press—33 East Minor Street, Emmaus, PA 18049 (215) 967-5171

National Committee for World Food Day—1001 22nd Street N.W., Washington, D.C. 20437 (202)653-2404

Eating With Joy

Allied with the African talent for hospitality is a capacity for celebration. The visitor who has been fortunate enough to share what was available among African friends, however desperate their circumstances, has gained an enduring lesson in living. Pausing for the serenity of a tea ceremony amid war in the Western Sahara, or joining a jubilant Easter feast in a bleak South African township, is seeing life itself affirmed in the common breaking of bread. Our wish is that you use this book in that same spirit of discovery, joy and wonder.

How To Use This Book

If you're a person who wants precise instructions and exact measurements in a recipe, *The Africa News Cookbook* should be reassuring. We've tried to explain the methods to be used and the amount of ingredients you'll need, and, where necessary, to describe the consistency and appearance of the finished product.

But cooking "by the book" is not the African way. So we urge you to discover how easily these recipes can be shaped to your own preferences. If you're a cook who enjoys experimenting, you'll be comfortable immediately. If you're not, by the time you've tried a number of these recipes several times, you may discover that you've acquired a new confidence in the kitchen that will carry over to other types of cooking.

By necessity, traditional African ways of eating have been a more responsible use of resources than the high-fat, excessively high-protein diets of much of the western world. Meat is more often a flavoring agent than the central item in a meal. Fruits and vegetables are generally fresh, naturally ripened, and less likely to be laced with toxic chemicals. In the absence of produce transported from places thousands of miles distant, what is eaten varies with the seasons.

Most of these recipes lend themselves to similarly thrifty, healthy practices. Let the list of ingredients be merely a guide; make soups, stews, curries and couscous with what you have on hand, or what is growing in your garden, or what is a good seasonal buy at your store. If you eat meat, try using smaller amounts than you normally would. Make carbohydrates a larger percentage of your diet—a practice that the newest nutritional research tells us is beneficial to health and not fattening, contrary to what we once were told.

Some dishes of Africa need ingredients or implements not readily available elsewhere—such as *berbere* to spice Ethiopian specialties, and a *couscousière* to steam couscous. In such cases, we offer alternative ways for you to approximate the real thing.

In its original conception, this book was to be a collection of *authentic* recipes, a guide to cooking as Africans do. It didn't take long for us to recognize how simplistic that aim was. Every cook has a highly individual way of combining similar raw materials into distinctive dishes. And urbanization has given rise to a greater variety of cooking methods, a larger reliance on semi-processed foods, and—like everywhere else in the world—to foreign influences in eating habits.

Where, we asked ourselves, would we draw the line of authenticity between a village woman pounding millet with a heavy wooden pestle and an office worker who buys his grain, already processed, at the supermarket? And what date would we use to draw the line on imported ingredients and methods? After all, some of the most widely-used, even staple foods of today came to the continent in the course of international contacts. Just as Ireland would not have the potato if there had been no trade in plant species, so Africa would not have the cassava, the tomato, the banana, the clove or the hot pepper. Yet these, along with more recent imports, have been incorporated into the culture and made Africa's own.

While we came to understand a society's way of eating as a living, evolving process, we also recognized the need to adapt the common dishes of rural Africa to the ingredients, kitchens and schedules of this book's likely users. What we have produced, therefore, is not a set of instructions for replicating what Africans eat. But it is an introduction to the cuisine of Africa that tries to reflect the spirit—and respect the skills—of those who create it.

The sections following will be helpful as you try these recipes. We recommend reading them before you begin. But the wonderful thing about most of the foods in this book is that they are so adaptable. Your version of *doro wat* may not be what you would find in Addis Ababa—but it is likely to be delicious all the same.

About grains and legumes

A diet that combines grains with legumes need have no other sources of protein to be healthful. Indeed, soybeans by themselves have complete protein, similar in structure to that found in milk. And soybeans have the advantage of being low in fat.

But most plant foods lack some of the essential amino acids that constitute complete protein. Because the amino acids in grains complement those in legumes, they are ideal partners in a balanced diet.

Traditional eating patterns in many parts of the globe, including Africa, take advantage of that complementarity. Rice and beans, beans and corn, lentils and millet, peas and wheat... Besides being good for you, these combinations offer almost limitless possibilities in tastes and textures.

In the field, too, grains and legumes (which much of the English-speaking world call *pulses*) sustain each other. Julius Nyerere, president of Tanzania for two decades, recounts how peasant villagers traditionally planted beans and corn together until foreign "experts" advised against the practice. Recently, Nyerere says, modern agronomy "discovered" that beans and corn—interplanted—grew faster, needed less weeding, repelled pests better and survived drought more readily than either planted alone. Now peasant farmers are advised to adopt the "new" method of planting mixed patches of corn and beans!

Frances Moore Lappé in her pioneering 1971 work, *Diet for a Small Planet*, called attention to the fact that an acre of grains can produce five times more protein than an acre devoted to raising cattle or other meat; an acre of legumes, 10 times more. Leafy greens are capable of producing an astonishing *15 times* as much protein as an acre devoted to meat production. So it is not surprising that African cooks, in countries short on arable land with good soil, have been inventive in developing recipes for grains and legumes and greens. For more information on vegetarian nutrition, consult such works as Lappé's book and *Laurel's Kitchen* published by Nilgiri Press.

Laurel's Kitchen has tips on buying and cooking various grains and legumes. It also reminds us that recent research contradicts earlier assumptions that protein complements must be consumed during the same sitting. Balancing the protein in your diet regularly, over a series of meals, is sufficient.

Here are some general rules for cooking legumes. Wash dried beans and peas thoroughly and skim off ones that float to the top, also discarding any that appear moldy. Soak overnight to cut a half hour or more from cooking time (although some people believe that pre-soaked legumes are a bit harder to digest). Cover the beans or peas with water, bring to a boil, then reduce heat and simmer until they are tender. This can take anywhere from less than an hour for lentils to over 3 hours for soybeans.

Remember that most dried legumes double in bulk when cooked.

About spices and herbs

Sitting unassumingly on the shelves of every supermarket and convenience store, the small jars and tins of cinnamon and cloves and coriander look less inspiring than the role they have played in world history. It was in search of spices, as much as of gold, that Columbus came to the Americas, that Marco Polo went to China, that Diaz rounded Africa.

But those European explorers were latecomers to the quest for culinary treasures. Two thousand years before Portugal's Bartholomao Diaz, Phoenician sailors sent by Egyptian King Necho rounded the Cape of Good Hope. Necho, who ruled from 610-594 B.C., dispatched the Phoenicians after trying in vain to dig a canal from the Mediterranean to the Red Sea—an attempt that

Herodotus reports took 120,000 Egyptian lives. Centuries before the Dutch East India Company attempted to monopolize the spice routes (sometimes burning tons of cinnamon to keep prices high), Arabian and Persian traders were plying the African and Asian coasts. So successfully did they conceal their sources that their Greek customers believed Ethiopia—merely a transit point—to be the home of cloves and cinnamon.

Sitting between the Pacific "spice islands" and Europe, Africa was destined to be significant to international commerce. For hundreds of years, Alexandria, Egypt, was the world's leading spice trading center. The exotic images evoked by such names as Zanzibar, Marrakesh and Timbuctu date from their importance as points of exchange for spices.

If we find it hard to credit spices as the inspiration for difficult, dangerous voyages, it may be because we are unfamiliar with their true potency. Those little jars are not the best way to discover the joys of spice cookery. Light, heat and exposure to air dissipate the volatile oils responsible for flavor. Grinding, because it exposes far more surfaces, further hastens the deterioration. So for spices and herbs, as for other ingredients, the fresher the better.

This doesn't mean you must always grind your own. It does suggest that you not store your spices in glass jars on an open shelf near your stove, however attractive they may be there. Find the coolest, darkest spot in your kitchen or pantry. Purchase small amounts, especially of those you use infrequently, and be sure to keep lids tightly closed.

But if you want to experience flavors at their fullest, search out *whole* spices at gourmet, ethnic or natural food shops. To prepare them, a grater and a simple grinding mechanism are all you need. Mortars and pestles of non-absorbent materials such as brass, marble or ceramic are good for all spices, as are two smooth stones—the larger as a base, the smaller, as a grindstone wielded by your hand. (Wooden mortars and pestles are excellent but not recommended for garlic and other pungent substances that might penetrate the wood. However, some of us have used our wooden ones happily, for years.) Most spices can also be ground in a blender or food processor, though for small amounts, the old-fashioned way is likely to be just as quick and easy. A little practice at crushing and grinding will make you adept.

There will be many times when, for one reason or another, you'll want to use pre-ground spices. A general rule-of-thumb is to use twice the amount of ground as you would of the fresh. No conversion is exact, nor can the dish be expected to taste the same. But even ground spices and dried herbs that have languished in your kitchen for far too long can transform an otherwise bland food. If you're trying to use less sodium, you may discover that more reliance on a diversity of seasonings will minimize your "salt tooth."

Don't be too timid, though. Many of us were taught to use spices so sparingly that they're barely detectable. You're probably more likely to use too little than too much. The amounts specified in these recipes, particularly for peppers, will give you milder results than you would find in Africa. Feel free to experiment.

Some Important Spices in African Cooking

Cardamom: Most Indian shops will have whole pods of "Elatchi" (*Elettaria cardamomum*), a perennial herb of the ginger family, and one of the most important curry flavorings. To use, peel away the fibrous capsule to get to the pungent reddish-brown seeds. Powder them just before use, if possible, because loss of flavor is rapid.

Cinnamon: "True" cinnamon (*Cinnamomum zeylanicum*) is native to Ceylon and the nearby Malabar coast of India. From the area around Saigon comes cassia (*Cinnamomum cassia*) a less delicately-flavored spice that used to be called "fake cinnamon," but today supplies most of the cinnamon used in the U.S. Both are the dried, inner bark of trees; you can tell them apart in stick form because true cinnamon is tightly rolled around itself while cassia is rolled from both ends towards the center, like a scroll. In Africa, its use is common in piquant as well as sweet dishes.

Cloves: Although thought to be native to the south Pacific, cloves today come mostly from the east African islands of Zanzibar and Pemba (part of Tanzania), and are also an important crop for Madagascar, further out in the Indian Ocean. If you visit Zanzibar, the smell of cloves will greet you upon your arrival, and stay with you in your hair and clothes and memory when you leave. Cinnamon and cloves are two spices that you will often choose to use pre-ground, especially in sweets. When you add them whole, for flavoring while cooking, be sure to remove them before serving the dish. (Tying small, whole spices in a cloth or putting them in a metal tea ball before adding them facilitates their removal.) Whole cloves are unopened buds of the clove tree (*Caryophyllus aromaticus*). Gently chewing one will freshen your breath, but be careful—the head is hot. For a milder aromatic, detach the head and use only the stem.

Coriander: This Mediterranean native (*Coriandrum sativum*) contributes to our tables both its leaves, used in soups, stews and salads, and its seeds, used whole in pickling spices and ground in curries. The fresh leaves, called *cilantro* or *Chinese parsley*, can often be found at Oriental food stores. What we call "seeds" are actually the plant's globular, ridged fruits. For true freshness, grow coriander in your garden or on a sunny windowsill. Because getting the leaves can mean a lengthy trip to a specialty store, Paula Wolfert in her book *Couscous and Other Good Food from Morocco*, gives instructions for making "coriander water" that can be frozen for later use in most recipes calling for fresh coriander. If you can't get the fresh leaves at all, try substituting parsley.

Cumin: Another curry ingredient, the herb cumin (*Cuminum cyminum*) originated in Egypt. Its fruit—yellowish-brown elongated ovals that are commonly called "cumin seeds"—are used both whole and ground in soups, stews, curries and fish and meat dishes.

Fennel: This European native (*Foeniculum vulgare*) is another herb that can prosper in North American gardens. The oblong seeds, with their anise-like flavor, are used whole or ground in soups, stews and sauces.

Fenugreek: Available whole or ground, the seeds of fenugreek (*Trigonella foenum-graecum*) are hard and pebble-like, and a bit difficult to grind at home. Their burnt-sugar flavor is prized for mango chutneys and pickles, for berbere and curry mixtures, and by north African Berbers for bread-making.

Garlic: Grown in nearly every part of the world, the bulb of garlic plants (*Allium sativum*) consists of a number of wedge-shaped "cloves," whose thin, transparent skin should be peeled away. Long cooking, as in African stews and curries, diminishes the biting quality of raw garlic, giving it a mild, almost nutty flavor. In dishes of north African and Indian origin, the pungency of garlic is often used to balance the sweetness of fruits or honey. In cultures where it is used extensively, garlic is widely valued for its medicinal properties. (For example, a tea made by steeping a dozen or more cloves in boiling water is drunk at bedtime to relieve congestion.) Since fresh garlic is nearly always available, you should seldom need to resort to garlic powder.

Ginger: The root, or rhizome of the ginger plant (*Zingiber officinale*) is used to flavor curries, stews and baked goods. Most of the fresh ginger available in North America is from Jamaica, although spice importers often use rhizomes from Nigeria or Sierra Leone for grinding. Many supermarkets as well as specialty shops now carry fresh ginger in the produce section. Break off and buy only as much as you will use within a couple of weeks, and refrigerate it to retard shriveling and mold formation. Before use, *carefully* pare off just the tough outer layer, since much of the essential oil is in tissues near the cork, or skin.

Mint: Among the many varieties of this perennial herb, spearmint (*Mentha spicata*) and peppermint (*Mentha piperita*) are the most common. If you plant them in your garden, they will proliferate beyond your ability to use them. (One solution is to grow them in pots. Another is to border a mint bed with up-ended bricks, dug into the soil so that only the top inch or so is exposed, to discourage the roots from spreading.) Use fresh sprigs in chutnies, sauces, drinks and salads. To dry mint for teas, harvest sprigs when the plants are blooming and let them dry in the sun for a day or two. Then tie them in bundles and hang in a warm place until the leaves can be easily crumbled.

Pepper: Hot peppers (*Capsicum*) and their ground spices are so central to cooking in much of Africa that they need their own section, *About peppers*. The most important thing when using any of the hot peppers is to remember not to touch your face—especially your eyes—while handling them. And always wash your hands thoroughly afterwards. For the fiercest varieties, protection of the skin with gloves is recommended!

Sesame: Across Africa, seeds of the sesame herb (*Sesamum indicum*), are most important for their oil. Sesame oil and sesame paste (*tahini*) can be found in Oriental food stores or in gourmet and specialty shops. The whole, hulled seeds (available in most supermarkets) are used in baking and as a garnish for north African stews.

Turmeric: In the tagines of north Africa and the curries of the south, a pinch of saffron, from the stigma of a Mediterranean crocus, can give character to a whole pot of food. But saffron, even in pinches, is frightfully expensive—as many as 5,000 flowers are needed to produce 1 ounce of the spice. So it has become conventional to substitute ground rhizomes of turmeric (*Curcuma longa*) wherever saffron is specified. While the flavor is somewhat different from saffron, turmeric imparts a similar orange-yellow tint to foods.

About peppers

Although foods in some parts of Africa tend to be bland, many regions of the continent share a liking for preparations that can be uncomfortably hot for the novice pepper-eater. From Addis Ababa to Dakar to Durban, stews, curries and even salads and vegetables can be so fiery as to seem, at first, indistinguishable from one another. Many travelers quickly become afficionadoes; others need gradually-increased exposure before learning to appreciate the spiciness.

Through the years, there has been considerable disagreement among botanists about correct classification of the numerous pepper varieties within the genus *Capsicum*. What is not a matter of dispute is that the hot ones should be respected. In his 1969 book, *The Story of Spices*, John W. Parry warns that the small African chilies, especially, should be handled with care. "They are particularly fiery, acrid and biting," he writes. "After handling these chilies the fingers should not be brought in touch with the eyes, and the chilies should not be tested by tasting."

But it isn't just the small peppers known as *Nigerian*, *Mombassa*, *Congo*, *Zanzibar* or simply *African* that pack a punch. We've known folks who purchased in an African market what they thought were ordinary sweet bell peppers, only to burn the skin on their hands as they tried to chop them. Dried hot peppers found in North American stores are likely to be somewhat less potent, but should still be handled cautiously.

An alternative to fresh or dried hot peppers when you can't buy or grow them, or you just want a short-cut, is a commercial ground pepper. Cayenne, made from the hottest small chilies, is truest to what you would use if you were cooking in Africa. Ground red pepper is generally somewhat milder. Chili powder is fine for certain uses, but should not be used interchangeably with cayenne, as it contains cumin, oregano, and garlic and onion powders in addition to pepper. A quick way to heat up your African concoctions, especially at the end, is to add Tabasco sauce, made from small Tabasco peppers that are almost as hot as the cayenne chilies. Tabasco is also a good way for bold diners to pep up their individual portions.

Among the mildest of the capsicum peppers is paprika, which can vary from sweet to quite pungent.

Interestingly, hot peppers are immigrants to Africa and India as well as to central Europe—all places where they have been adopted enthusiastically. Although they are now cultivated around the world, capsicums are native to tropical America.

About shrimp

Because fresh shrimp often are sold uncleaned, you may need to know how to handle any you buy. The first step is a thorough washing in cool water. Then, if you want to shell them, simply hold the shell in the fingers of one hand and pull the shrimp out with the other hand. (However, the tail shells add flavor during cooking; see the recipe on page 85.)

Either before or after cooking, you should remove the thin, dark-colored vein that runs along the curved underside of each shrimp. This is easy to do with a small sharp knife. For further information about choosing and preparing shellfish or other seafood, consult a standard reference such as *Joy of Cooking*.

About peeling

Many African cooks are fastidious about peeling tomatoes, partly because long stewing and re-heating can toughen the skins. We never bother to peel ours, regardless of what the recipe requires, but the process is not difficult. Simply plunge tomatoes into boiling water for a minute or two, lift them out with a slotted spoon, and then dip them into ice-cold water for a moment. The skins should slip off easily.

The same technique often works for things besides tomatoes (see the recipe for sautéed almonds on page 28). Sweet bell peppers are sometimes peeled by charring them over coals or under a broiler until the skin begins to flake.

This book makes the assumption that you will always peel onions, garlic, ginger and such fruits as oranges, bananas and plantains. Potatoes, like most vegetables, may be peeled or not, according to your personal preference. In general, we recommend not peeling if you grow your own or can buy organically-grown produce. Otherwise, you'll have to choose between retaining the nutrients in the skins and avoiding the residues of pesticides and herbicides that may be on them.

About frying

As sedentary Westerners have become more conscious of the role of diet in maintaining health, frying has lost favor as a method of food preparation. Africans, who are likely to expend many more calories in vigorous work, may suffer less from the fat intake associated with frying. In any case, in predominately rural countries where ovens are rare, such alternatives as baking or broiling may not be options.

Where ovens *are* available, a number of the foods that traditionally would be fried can be baked, broiled or steamed instead. But even those of us who are serious about cutting fat consumption are tempted by the occasional fried treat—like bananas rolled in pastry (page 149).

Most foods, even those meant to be fried in deep fat, can be cooked successfully in a heavy pan with a shallow coating of oil on the bottom. But they will be lightest and least greasy when skillfully cooked in hot, deep fat—a method that takes considerable practice to master.

Deep-fat frying is an art best learned in your own kitchen at a tender age. If you weren't fortunate enough to have that sort of early training, don't despair. After reading this section you can achieve passable results on your first try. The easiest way is to have a frying thermometer and a gas stove, both of which are helpful in maintaining a consistent temperature. Without them you'll have more trial and error, but even your errors should be tasty, if not as pretty as you'd like.

You'll need a fat with a high smoking temperature such as safflower, peanut, or soybean oil. Use a heavy pot, large enough so that several inches of oil will fill it no more than half full (an important safety precaution). If your stove is electric, make sure that the bottom of the pot is flat; otherwise you won't have enough contact with the burner to assure an adequate or steady temperature.

Heat the oil gradually to 350-365° for moist batters and doughs, and to 365-375° for balls or croquettes. (If the weather is chilly, heat your thermometer in warm water and then dry it well before testing the temperature.) Accuracy is important, because if the oil is too hot, the outside of your food will burn before the insides are cooked; if it's too cool, the fried food will become greasy. What you want to aim for is a temperature that will crisp and seal the surface immediately, but won't overcook it. If you don't have a thermometer, drop in a 1-inch-square cube of bread. It should turn golden brown in 60 seconds at 350-365° and in 40 seconds at 365-375°. Asian cooks test oil temperature by dropping in a dry rice noodle. If it puffs up within a few seconds, the oil is ready for most frying.

Cook only 2 or 3 pieces at the same time, turning them if necessary to brown both sides. Between batches, let the oil heat to the proper temperature again. If you try to cook too much at once, moisture in the food may cause the oil to bubble over the edge of the pot, or the oil temperature may drop too rapidly.

Experience will soon help you improve your technique. When cooking banana fritters (page 144), for example, each quarter-cupful that you ladle in should sink and then quickly rise to the top, all in one piece. Too-hot oil will cause the batter to spatter into several bits. But don't worry overmuch if your fritters have a scraggly appearance; some people like the crisp, ragged edges best of all.

Warning: you should always exercise extreme caution when cooking with hot fat. Don't drop solid items into it; lower them so that there is no splashing. Don't use any wet implements because water causes oil to splatter, and you could be burned. Pour moist batters into hot oil quickly but carefully, and stand well back from the pot.

As you cook, periodically skim out any errant crumbs or pieces of batter with a slotted spoon. And have clean cloths or paper towels ready for each newly-cooked batch. We prefer draining fried foods on absorbent cloths that can be laundered and pressed into service again and again.

Oil used for frying should be strained through a porous cloth, then bottled and refrigerated. You can remove any odors it may have absorbed by heating it to 375° and frying a couple of small pieces of fresh ginger in it before straining. Oil may be reused until it darkens in color or smokes when heated (which happens eventually because impurities from previous fryings lower the smoking temperature).

One further note about cooking with oil or butter: a number of the recipes in these pages call for significant amounts of fat, even when frying is not the cooking method. If you need to reduce your fat consumption, you should feel free to use less than the instructions specify.

Africa's Ethnolinguistic Diversity

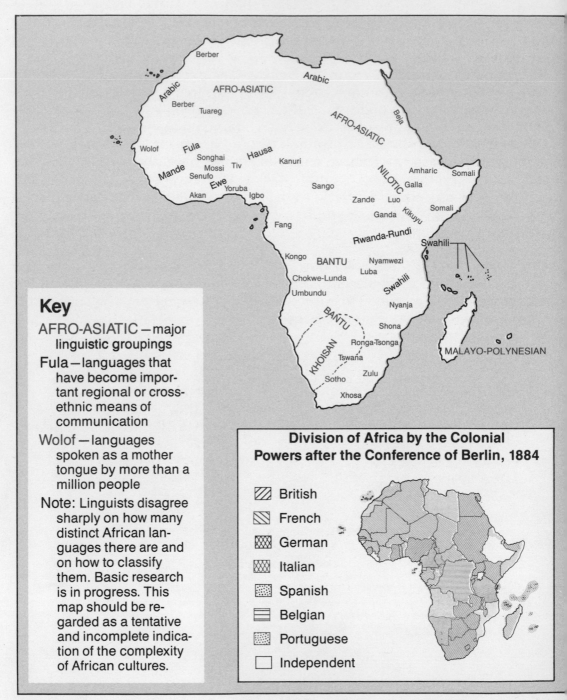

Berber

Arabic

AFRO-ASIATIC

Arabic

Berber

Tuareg

AFRO-ASIATIC

Beja

Wolof

Fula

Songhai

Mande

Mossi

Tiv

Hausa

Senufo

Ewe

Yoruba

Akan

Igbo

Kanuri

Sango

Zande

Luo

Ganda

Kikuyu

NILOTIC

Amharic

Galla

Somali

Somali

Fang

Rwanda-Rundi

Swahili

Kongo

BANTU

Nyamwezi

Luba

Chokwe-Lunda

Swahili

Umbundu

Nyanja

BANTU

Shona

KHOISAN

Tswana

Ronga-Tsonga

MALAYO-POLYNESIAN

Sotho

Zulu

Xhosa

Key

AFRO-ASIATIC — major linguistic groupings

Fula — languages that have become important regional or cross-ethnic means of communication

Wolof — languages spoken as a mother tongue by more than a million people

Note: Linguists disagree sharply on how many distinct African languages there are and on how to classify them. Basic research is in progress. This map should be regarded as a tentative and incomplete indication of the complexity of African cultures.

Division of Africa by the Colonial Powers after the Conference of Berlin, 1884

- British
- French
- German
- Italian
- Spanish
- Belgian
- Portuguese
- Independent

These maps are derived from a Mercator projection which has been used here because of its familiarity.

The Nations of Africa and Their Capitals

ALGERIA (Algiers)
ANGOLA (Luanda)
BENIN (Porto-Novo)
BOTSWANA (Gaborone)
BURKINA FASO (Ouagadougou)
BURUNDI (Bujumbura)
CAMEROON (Yaoundé)
CAPE VERDE (Praia)
CENTRAL AFRICAN REPUBLIC
   (Bangui)
CHAD (N'djamena)
COMORO ISLANDS (Moroni)
CONGO REPUBLIC (Brazzaville)
DJIBOUTI (Djibouti)
EGYPT (Cairo)
EQUATORIAL GUINEA (Malabo)
ETHIOPIA (Addis Ababa)
GABON (Libreville)
GAMBIA (Banjul)
GHANA (Accra)
GUINEA (Conakry)
GUINEA-BISSAU (Bissau)
IVORY COAST (Abidjan)
KENYA (Nairobi)
LESOTHO (Maseru)
LIBERIA (Monrovia)
LIBYA (Tripoli)
MADAGASCAR (Antananarivo)

MALAWI (Lilongwe)
MALI (Bamako)
MAURITANIA (Nouakchott)
MAURITIUS (Port Louis)
MOROCCO (Rabat)
MOZAMBIQUE (Maputo)
NAMIBIA (Windhoek)
NIGER (Niamey)
NIGERIA (Abuja)*
RWANDA (Kigali)
SÃO TOMÉ AND PRINÇIPÉ (São
   Tomé)
SENEGAL (Dakar)
SEYCHELLES (Victoria)
SIERRA LEONE (Freetown)
SOMALIA (Mogadishu)
SOUTH AFRICA (Pretoria)**
SUDAN (Khartoum)
SWAZILAND (Mbabane)
TANZANIA (Dar es Salaam)
TOGO (Lomé)
TUNISIA (Tunis)
UGANDA (Kampala)
WESTERN SAHARA (El Aaiun)
ZAIRE (Kinshasa)
ZAMBIA (Lusaka)
ZIMBABWE (Harare)

*Lagos is the largest city and the principal port
**administrative capital

The Canary Islands, off Morocco's southwest coast, are a Spanish possession that is not officially recognized as an African country.

Spices, Sauces
and Condiments

African food ranges from bland, staple cornmeal porridges to curries so hot that the only taste an untrained palate can distinguish is *fire*. In between is a whole range of flavors and sensations. In many cases, it is not only the spice mixtures featured in the main dish, but also the sideshow attractions of sauces and condiments that give meals their character.

Little more needs to be said. Words are inadequate to describe these savories, and once tasted they speak for themselves.

Peppers

Ethiopian and Mozambican dishes would be inconceivable without the spicy concoctions that give a characteristic flavor, as well as heat, to the food. While each cook has an individual method and blend of spices, these berbere and piri piri recipes are typical. They will keep well for several weeks if stored in a cool, dark place, and for six months or more if refrigerated. Try using them in stews and vegetables as well as in the recipes that specify them.

Berbere   Ethiopia
Hot Pepper Seasoning

Makes 1 cup. Ethiopian berbere includes spices and herbs not readily available elsewhere, but the two versions that follow are reasonable adaptations. You also may want to add some crushed, fresh mint leaves (in place of Ethiopian Bishop's Weed).

2 tsp. cumin seeds
4 whole cloves
6 cardamom pods
½ tsp. whole black pepper
¼ tsp. whole allspice
1 tsp. whole fenugreek seeds
½ cup dried shallots
3 oz. long red dried chilies
3-6 small, dried hot chili peppers
½ tsp. ground ginger
¼ tsp. turmeric
2 tsp. salt

In a small frying pan, combine the cumin seeds, cloves, cardamom pods, black pepper, allspice, and fenugreek. Cook over medium-low heat, stirring, until lightly toasted, about 1 minute. Place in a blender, add shallots, and whirl until finely ground. Discard stems and seeds from chilies. Break up the pods and process until ground. Combine with the toasted seasonings and the remaining spices.

2

Berbere   Ethiopia

Makes about 1½ cups

1 tsp. ground ginger
½ tsp. ground cardamom
½ tsp. ground coriander
½ tsp. ground fenugreek seeds
½ tsp. grated nutmeg
¼ tsp. ground cloves
¼ tsp. cinnamon
¼ tsp. allspice
2 tblsp. salt
1¼ cup cayenne pepper
½ cup paprika
1 tsp. freshly ground black
   pepper

In a heavy saucepan, toast the following ground spices together over low heat 4 to 5 minutes: ginger, cardamom, coriander, fenugreek, nutmeg, cloves, cinnamon, and allspice. Shake or stir to prevent burning.

Add the salt, cayenne pepper, paprika, and freshly ground black pepper and continue toasting and stirring 10 to 15 minutes. Cool and store in tightly covered glass jar. This will keep in the refrigerator 5 or 6 months.

Berbere   Ethiopia

Use this mixture for individual dishes when you don't have a supply of berbere on hand. Makes 3 heaping tablespoons.

1 tsp. ground ginger
3 tblsp. cayenne pepper
¼ tsp. ground cloves
½ tsp. cinnamon

Combine the spices.

3

Piripiri   Mozambique

What curries are to foods of Asian origin, piripiri is to the cuisine of Mozambique. Originally the name of a small, red capsicum pepper, piripiri today can refer to any of the various hot, spicy dishes made with the fresh pepper itself or with the dried, ground powder it produces.

Recipes in the seafood and chicken chapters of this book call for piripiri both as a marinade and as a sauce, but these mixtures can be used successfully with almost any kind of meat. Shrimp, prawns and chicken are the favorite choices in Mozambique, and charcoal grilling is the preferred method of cooking. This recipe is enough for 3-4 lbs. of chicken or fish. When making large quantities, a food processor or blender is convenient; for small amounts, a mortar and pestle is both fast and easy to clean.

4 red peppers, crushed or 2
   heaping tsp. cayenne pepper
¼ tsp. salt
juice of 2 medium-size lemons
2 cloves garlic, crushed
6 sprigs parsley, chopped
1 cup butter or oil

For a marinade, combine all the ingredients except butter in a bowl with meat or seafood. Stir to coat each piece well. If you'll be cooking within a couple of hours, let the mixture sit at room temperature; otherwise, cover and refrigerate. Marinating overnight allows all the flavors to blend nicely.

To make a sauce for basting, combine everything, including the butter. If you have made a marinade, you can use the liquid left in the bowl after the pieces of meat are removed, but it may be necessary to add a bit more of each ingredient in roughly the same proportions as before.

To make a table sauce for the cooked meat, prepare a fresh mixture of all the ingredients and heat it gently for five minutes before serving. As a variation for basting chicken, substitute 1 cup of coconut milk (see recipe, page 7) for the lemon juice.

Curry Powder   Southern Africa

The curries of southern and eastern Africa, like their older Asian cousins, are not made with curry powder. Instead, each dish gets its own tailored blend of freshly-ground herbs and spices— as many as 50 and as few as 8, depending on the effect the cook wants to achieve and the resources at hand.

In this book, the authentic curry recipes specify individual spices, but curry powder does occur as a flavoring agent in other foods. And there are times when even the most serious cook wants a shortcut. To substitute a pre-blended powder for the spices in curry recipes, simply total the amounts of the spices and add a similar amount of curry powder. If you make your own regularly, it will be fresher and better than any commercial preparation you can buy.

In these three mixtures, ingredient amounts are given in ratios. For example, to make the mild variation you would use 1 part cayenne pepper, 12 parts cardamom, 24 parts coriander and so on. The parts, of course, can be any volume you choose— tablespoons, ounces or pounds! For smaller amounts, you might use ¼ teaspoon cayenne to 3 teaspoons cardamom to 6 teaspoons coriander. Make only as much as you expect to use during the next 3 or 4 months and store tightly covered in a cool, dark place.

Although an increasing number of supermarkets carry whole spices, you will find that spices tend to be fresher at an ethnic or specialty grocery. Crush them with a grindstone, a mortar and pestle or a blender or food processer. Don't expect the result to be as finely-ground or as uniform as purchased powders, but the aroma will be far more seductive. If you prefer, you can use ground rather than whole spices.

For a mild curry powder:

1 cayenne	2 fennel
12 cardamom	10 fenugreek
24 coriander	5 white or black pepper
4 cloves	32 turmeric
10 cumin	

For a hot curry powder:

6 cayenne	2 fennel
12 cardamom	4 fenugreek
22 coriander	7 ginger
2 cloves	5 white or black pepper
10 cumin	30 turmeric

5

A curry powder for fish:

2 cayenne
32 coriander
10 cumin
4 fennel

10 fenugreek
10 white or black pepper
32 turmeric

Ghurum Masala   Southern Africa

To pep up the flavor of a curry after it's cooked, Ghurum Masala is stirred in before serving. It should not be substituted for the curry spices added during cooking.

½ lb. ground coriander
2 oz. ground cumin
½ oz. ground cloves
½ oz. ground cayenne pepper
½ oz. ground cinnamon

Mix the spices well, and spread on a flat baking sheet. Toast in a 250° oven, being careful not to let them burn—about 10 minutes. Stir once or twice during toasting. Let cool. Store in tightly covered jars in a cool, dry place.

Coconuts

Although the coconut milk or cream called for in a number of these recipes can be made from packaged, dried coconut, you will find it worthwhile to make your own. Look for fresh coconuts in the produce section of your grocery or in specialty shops. The best test for freshness is to shake the coconut and listen for a definite sloshing inside—the more liquid you hear the better. If there is no sound, don't buy that coconut because it's likely to be dried up and sour.

Once you have a coconut, you'll need to open it. Drain it first by hammering a nail or an icepick into two of the black spots, or eyes; then, through one of them, pour out and discard the liquid. (If you have access to coconuts fresh from a tree, you will find the liquid good for drinking or cooking. But in older coconuts, it tends to acquire an unpleasant after-taste, especially when heated.)

There are two common methods for loosening the white meat from the shell. One is to tap firmly with a mallet or a hammer all around the outside.

Then lay the coconut on a hard surface and give it a sharp blow to crack it open. The other way is to bake the whole coconut in a 350° oven for about an hour, until the shell begins to split. Sometimes neither approach works and you'll need to pry the meat loose from each piece with a knife. Remove the brown skin clinging to the meat with a paring knife or carrot peeler. When you're pressed for time or don't have a hammer, you can open a coconut by throwing it against a brick or cement floor. If you haven't drained it, lay down newspapers beforehand to absorb the liquid.

All this is not as formidable as it sounds, and can be fun, especially if you have the help of children, who seem to love every part of the process.

Coconut Milk

Makes about 3 cups

fresh white meat of 1 coconut

First, grate the meat by hand, or process it in a blender or food processor. The next step is to extract the flavorful moisture from the gratings. Africans often use a conical woven basket, whose function you can duplicate by lining a bowl with cotton cloth such as cheesecloth or an old, clean diaper. The liner should be big enough to drape over the sides of the bowl. Dump the grated coconut onto the cloth, then pour about 1 cup of boiling water over it. When cool enough to handle, gather the edges of the cloth and lift it above the bowl, wringing with both hands to squeeze out the milky liquid, which you should pour off and save. Repeat the process three times.

Because the first pressing will be the most concentrated, if your recipe calls for less than 3 cups, keep each squeezing separate and use the earlier ones first. Anything left over can be used for cooking vegetables or rice.

Coconut Cream

In common usage, coconut cream may be two different things, either of which will work in recipes. Sometimes, "cream" simply refers to the first squeezing. In other places, the word is used to mean the thicker layer that forms on top of chilled coconut milk. Both coconut cream and coconut milk will keep for 2 or 3 days when refrigerated, or for several months in a freezer. In either case, cover the container securely.

Butters

Throughout Africa, people churn butter from the milk of their own cows, goats or camels. Its use gives food a taste not easily duplicated in the United States, where fresh, creamery butter is a thing of the past.

Without prompt refrigeration and careful packaging, butter is subject to spoilage and to the absorption of unpleasant odors. And because of the milk solids it contains, it has a low scorching temperature that limits its usefulness in cooking. Although the addition of salt improves shelf life, salted butter still burns easily, and it, too, must be kept chilled.

The African answer to both problems is removal of the milk solids through a process called *clarifying*. Clarified butter keeps well, even at room temperature, and is considered a must for the stews of Ethiopia and Morocco, for the seafood sauces of coastal areas, and for the Indian-origin dishes of east and southern Africa.

Although many Americans stay away from butter for economic and health reasons, we prefer to avoid the additives in margarine. A good compromise is the common African practice of combining butter with oil. Our method is to put equal parts of butter and a polyunsaturated oil such as safflower in a blender or food processor, letting them sit until the butter is slightly soft. (It's easier to get all the lumps out if neither ingredient is too cold.) Then we whir them for a minute or two to get a smooth, somewhat thick liquid. When refrigerated, the mixture solidifies to a firm, but easily-spreadable consistency that makes it perfect for the table. It can be used with good results in almost any recipe—though you may still want to choose pure butter for cakes and pastries.

You also may use a proportion of oil in recipes calling for clarified butter. The accepted method is to use 40-60 per cent butter, and to add both butter and oil directly to the dish being prepared.

Clarified Butter

Makes just under 1 cup

8 oz. (2 sticks) butter

Cut butter into pieces and melt in a saucepan over low heat. With a slotted spoon, skim off the butterfat that will foam to the top. Remove the pan from heat. After letting it sit a few minutes, slowly pour off the clear liquid, leaving behind the residue of milk solids that has settled to the bottom. You now have clarified butter that will last at least 2 to 3 weeks if kept cold.

Where refrigeration is less common, as in most of Africa, the butter is simmered over lowest heat, uncovered and undisturbed, for 40-50 minutes. Then the clear liquid is strained two or three times by pouring it through clean, finely-woven cloth into a bowl. This removes any traces of milk solids that would cause rancidity. Strained this way, clarified butter will stay fresh, even at room temperature, for several weeks. Like ordinary butter, it may be frozen for later use.

Niter Kebbeh   Ethiopia
Clarified Butter with Spices

Makes about 2 cups

1 lb. butter
4 tblsp. onion, chopped
1½ tblsp. finely chopped garlic
2 tsp. fresh ginger, grated
½ tsp. turmeric
2-4 cardamom seeds, crushed
1-inch piece cinnamon
2-3 whole cloves
⅛ tsp. ground nutmeg

Slowly melt the butter in a saucepan, then bring to a boil. When the top is covered with foam, add the other ingredients and simmer uncovered on lowest heat until the surface is transparent and milk solids are on the bottom (45 to 60 minutes). Pour off the clear liquid and strain through a double layer of damp cheesecloth, discarding the spices and solids. Refrigerate. If strained a second and third time, mixture will keep well either chilled or at room temperature for 2-3 months.

Pickles and Preserves

Africa's wonderful fresh fruits and vegetables are preserved most often by drying, but there is also a tradition of pickling—either in oil or in vinegar. Southern Africa's vinegar-preserved chutneys and oil-preserved atjars carry the preparation of those condiments to a high art. Although they originated in India, Indonesia and Malaysia, they have been so adapted over the years that the recipes here are truly indigenous. Our versions allow only for short-term, refrigerated storage. If you want longer-lasting preserves, process them according to standard procedures for safe canning. Note that several of these foods must be started a few days ahead of the time that you want to serve them.

Pickled Lemons   Morocco

Makes about 7 dozen lemon wedges.

20-24 small, thin-skinned
   lemons
¼ cup coarse pickling salt

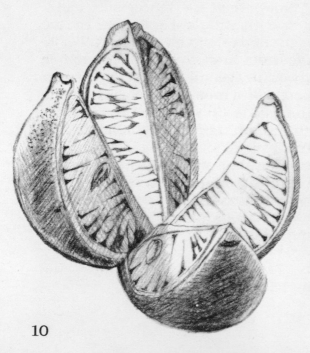

Quarter each lemon, but don't cut all the way through; leave the slices attached on one end. Sprinkle a pinch of salt in the bottom of a large, earthenware crock and another few pinches on the lemons. Pack the slices into the container until they are crushed sufficiently to nearly cover themselves in juice. (If they don't produce enough, you may need to squeeze 2 to 4 other lemons, and add their juice to the crock.) Cover with a lid or plate and let stand, preferably in a cool place. After 4 days stir the lemons, and re-cover tightly with a doubled or tripled piece of plastic wrap. Fasten with a rubber band around the jar's neck. Leave undisturbed for at least one month. Rinse the lemons in cold water before adding to recipes or serving.

Green Bean Atjar   South Africa
Green Bean Pickles

Makes about 3 pints

2 lbs. stringless or strung green
   beans
2 tblsp. salt
2 cups oil
1 tsp. fenugreek
1 tsp. turmeric
2 tblsp. curry powder
2 chili peppers, chopped, or 2
   tsp. cayenne pepper

Blanch the beans to retain a bright green color by dipping them into boiling water for 2 minutes. Lift out or drain immediately, and rinse in cold water. Drain again, gently mix in the salt, and let the beans sit for 2 or 3 hours. Meanwhile, combine the oil and all the spices, and bring to a boil while stirring. Remove from heat to cool. When the beans have sat long enough, pack them snugly into clean jars and pour in the spiced oil to cover. Cool and refrigerate. After 2 or 3 days they will be ready to serve. Without processing, the beans will last about a month.

Brinjal Blatjang   South Africa
Eggplant Chutney

2 lbs. eggplant
1 tblsp. ginger, grated
1 tblsp. garlic, pounded
¾ cup vinegar
6 chili peppers, slit or 4 tsp.
   cayenne pepper
1 cup vegetable oil
1 tsp. fenugreek
1 tsp. mustard seeds
¼ tsp. cumin seeds, pounded
1 tsp. turmeric
2 tblsp. sugar
4 tsp. salt

Peel the eggplant and cut into one-inch cubes. Cover the pieces with cold water in a bowl, and let them sit while you mix the ginger, garlic, vinegar and chilies and pound or blend them to a paste. Next, heat the oil in an enamel or aluminum pot, and stir in the fenugreek, mustard, cumin, turmeric, sugar and salt. When the mustard seeds stop sputtering, mix in the spice paste. Drain the eggplant, add it to the pot, and simmer until tender. Occasionally stir in the oil that will float to the top. Spoon into clean jars, cool and refrigerate. The chutney will keep for about a month.

11

Apple, Tomato and Raisin Chutney

South Africa

4 lbs. large ripe tomatoes
3 large onions, peeled and
  chopped
2½ cups cider vinegar
2½ cups brown sugar
1 tblsp. mustard seeds, crushed
½ tsp. cayenne pepper
1 tblsp. salt
4 tsp. fresh ginger, grated
1½ cup raisins
1½ tsp. coriander
10 whole cloves
3 lbs. tart green apples

Quarter the tomatoes and puree them in a blender or food processor, or mash well with a fork. Simmer them, along with the onions, in a heavy pot. Stir occasionally, adding a bit of water if the tomatoes have not produced enough liquid to prevent the mixture from sticking. After 45 minutes, add all the remaining ingredients except apples, and cook until you have a thick paste suitable for spooning alongside curries (the time can vary greatly). Add the apples and cook another half hour. Spoon into clean jars, cap, and refrigerate when cool. The chutney will keep 4 to 6 weeks.

Mint Chutney

Tanzania

This coastal east African-style chutney is popular for its unusual combination of flavors. It requires fresh coriander, usually called cilantro in the U.S., which is available in larger supermarkets or in specialty stores. The amounts of ingredients are approximate and variable. Experiment, and make your own personal variation. Fresh-mint chutney is especially good with fish and chicken curries.

½ cup fresh mint
½ cup fresh coriander leaves
a handful of cashew nuts or
  peanuts
3 or 4 cloves of garlic
juice of 2 limes
1 to 3 tsp. coriander seeds
1 tblsp. sugar
⅛ to ¼ tsp. salt
1 mildly-hot pepper
a pinch of cayenne pepper

Combine all ingredients in a blender or food processor and whirl until well mixed. Scrape the mixture into a clean jar and cover tightly. It will last for 3 or 4 weeks in the refrigerator.

Apricot Blatjang   South Africa
Apricot Chutney

Makes about 2 cups. You can purchase the peeled, slivered almonds you'll need, but more economical is to buy raw almonds by the pound. When boiled in water for 2 to 3 minutes, their skins will slip off easily.

1¼ cups dried apricots, quartered
¼ cup onions, diced
¼ cup raisins
½ cup vinegar
2 tblsp. sugar
2 cloves garlic, sliced
1 tblsp. fresh ginger, peeled and chopped
1 dried hot pepper, crumbled, or 1 tsp. cayenne pepper
1 tsp. coriander, ground
1 tsp. salt
¼ cup slivered almonds, peeled

Combine the apricots, onions, raisins, vinegar and sugar in a saucepan with enough water to cover, about 1 cup. Bring to a boil, stirring frequently. When sugar is dissolved, reduce heat and simmer until fruit is soft and the liquid has the consistency of honey, about 15 minutes. Add more water if mixture becomes too thick. Meanwhile, pound garlic, ginger and pepper to a paste with grindstones or a mortar and pestle. Mix with coriander and salt. (Or puree all the spices in a blender or food processor.) When apricot mixture is ready, remove from heat and stir in the spices and almonds. Spoon into glass jars. Cool, then cover and refrigerate. Keeps about 2 weeks. Serve with curries.

Manga de Conserva   Cape Verde
Preserved Mangoes

Makes about 1½ cups

2-3 unripe mangoes, diced
   (about 2 lbs. total)
1 tsp. salt
⅛-¼ cup vinegar (depending on
   your fondness for tartness)
¾ cup oil
1 hot red pepper, crushed, or 2
   tsp. cayenne pepper
fresh ginger, about 2 inches
   square, grated and crushed

Choose mangoes that are not yet soft. In a saucepan, dissolve salt in a cup of warm water, then add mango, bringing just to a boil. With a slotted spoon, immediately transfer mango pieces to a glass or ceramic bowl. Combine the remaining ingredients and stir into the mango. When each piece is well coated, spoon into glass jars, pouring in any leftover brine. Refrigerate. Chill for 2 or 3 days before serving as a pickle or condiment.

Banana Condiment   Zaire

Makes about 1 cup

4-6 overripe bananas
juice and grated peel of 1 large
    or 2 small lemons
¼ cup sugar

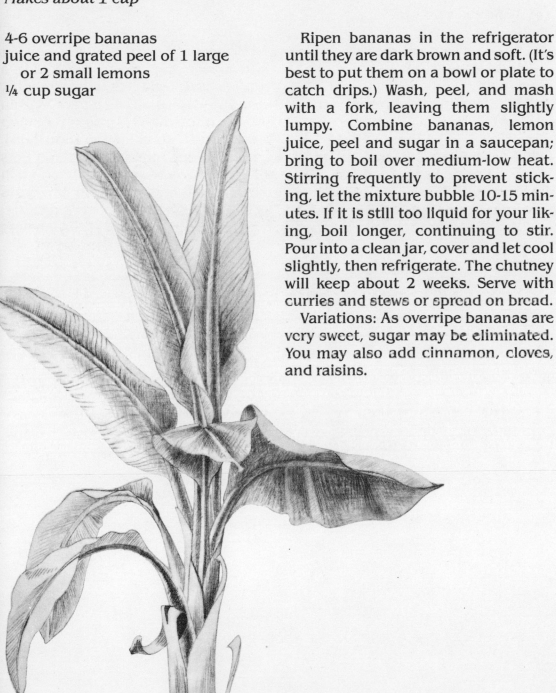

Ripen bananas in the refrigerator until they are dark brown and soft. (It's best to put them on a bowl or plate to catch drips.) Wash, peel, and mash with a fork, leaving them slightly lumpy. Combine bananas, lemon juice, peel and sugar in a saucepan; bring to boil over medium-low heat. Stirring frequently to prevent sticking, let the mixture bubble 10-15 minutes. If it is still too liquid for your liking, boil longer, continuing to stir. Pour into a clean jar, cover and let cool slightly, then refrigerate. The chutney will keep about 2 weeks. Serve with curries and stews or spread on bread.

Variations: As overripe bananas are very sweet, sugar may be eliminated. You may also add cinnamon, cloves, and raisins.

Soups, Snacks and Appetizers

Except for the northern and southern rims of the continent, meals tend to be one-dish affairs, and snacks frequently substitute for a formal lunch or dinner. Most of the recipes in this chapter can function as a first course or as the centerpiece of a meal, depending on the amount served.

Soups

The bones and meat called for in these hearty soups are not essential, although if you leave them out you may want to add a cube or two of vegetable bouillon for flavor. All the soups lend themselves to experimentation with spices and vegetables of your own choosing. And all are true "convenience foods" that can be made ahead and re-heated. Or they can be prepared quickly by pre-cooking the legumes. It's also easy to make a few servings more or less by varying the amount of water used.

Hkatenkwan   Ghana
Groundnut Soup

Serves 4-6. Groundnut (peanut) soups and stews are probably the first foods that come to mind when west African cooking is mentioned. You may grind your own fresh peanuts if you wish, but using peanut butter is easier. Be sure to choose a kind without sugar or other additives; health food shops are likely sources if your grocery store doesn't carry a pure, unadulterated brand. The soup is good over rice or fufu.(See recipes in Grains and Bread chapter.)

1 small chicken or 2 lbs. chicken
   parts
1-inch piece of ginger
1½ cups onion, chopped
2 tblsp. tomato paste
1 cup tomatoes, chopped
salt and pepper to taste
1 cup peanut butter
1 medium-size eggplant, diced
2 cups okra or 1 8-oz. package
   frozen okra

Boil chicken and ginger in 6 cups water with ½ cup of the onion for 15-20 minutes. Meanwhile, in a large soup pot, fry the tomato paste in oil for 3 minutes, stirring briskly to mix. Add tomatoes and the rest of the onion. Sauté at a moderately hot temperature until onions are transparent. Add chicken with its cooking water, plus salt and pepper.

After 5 minutes, spoon out about ¼ cup of the hot broth and mix it with the peanut butter to make a paste. Add, along with the eggplant and okra, to the pot. Cook until chicken and vegetables are tender. Remove ginger piece before serving the soup.

Green Pea Soup

Southern Africa

Serves 4

1 onion, chopped
2 tblsp. oil or clarified butter
(see recipe, page 9)
½ lb. soup bones
½ tsp. ginger
½ tsp. garlic
2 tsp. salt
3-6 whole peppercorns
1 tsp. turmeric
2-3 tsp. ground coriander
1-3 tsp. cumin
2 chili peppers, crushed
½ tsp. chili powder
3-6 whole cloves
1 stick cinnamon
2 cardamom pods, crushed
1 cup dried green split peas

2 tomatoes, chopped
1 tsp. ghurum masala (see
recipe, page 6)
2 shallots, chopped (optional)

In a large soup pot, fry the onions in oil until light brown. Stir in bones and all the spices until oil is well distributed. Toss in the peas and tomatoes, stir again, and cook for 5 minutes over moderate heat. Then boil 4-6 cups water and pour into the soup pot. Cover and simmer until peas are tender, 2-3 hours. Before serving, take pot from heat and remove bones, cloves and peppercorns. Stir in ghurum masala and garnish with shallots.

Chorba 'dess

Algeria

Lentil Soup

Serves 4

¼ lb. stew veal or veal bones
1 large onion, chopped
2 tsp. ground coriander
2 tblsp. olive oil
1 cup dried lentils
1 large potato
1 large carrot
salt and pepper to taste

Stir the meat, onions and coriander in moderately hot oil in a large soup pot. Meanwhile, pour boiling water over the lentils and let them swell for several minutes.

When meat and onions are thoroughly brown, drain the lentils and add them to the pot along with about 4 cups of fresh water. Reduce heat to simmer and toss in the vegetables. Cook until vegetables are tender—about an hour—adding salt and pepper near the end. You may also want to add more coriander.

Chorba Hamra
Spicy Vegetable Soup

Algeria

Serves 4-6

¼ lb. (1 stick) butter or oil
½ lb. lamb, cubed
1 large onion, minced
2 tsp. ground coriander
½ tsp. cayenne pepper
pinch of black pepper
pinch of cinnamon
1 tsp. salt
1 lb. tomatoes
1 large potato
1 large carrot
1 medium zucchini
1 stalk celery
handful of dried chickpeas
¼ lb. vermicelli (thin spaghetti)
1 lemon, thinly sliced

Melt the butter or heat the oil in a large, deep pot. Combine the lamb, onion, coriander, peppers, cinnamon and salt and stir into the pot. Purée, or mash, the tomatoes and toss them in. (If you prefer them peeled and seeded, see *About peeling* in the Introduction.) Meanwhile, thinly slice the potato, carrot, zucchini and celery. When the meat is well browned, add 6-8 cups of water and bring to a boil. Toss in the sliced vegetables and the chickpeas. Cover, reduce heat to simmer and cook until everything is tender. Add water as necessary to make the amount of soup you need. A few minutes before serving, return mixture to a boil and stir in the pasta. Taste to see if you should shake in a bit more coriander, salt or pepper. When the noodles are cooked, serve in bowls with a slice of lemon floating on top.

Squash Soup   Mozambique

Serves 4-6. The Mozambican who inspired this recipe cooks it differently each time he makes it, depending on what is fresh in the market and what spices he can get. The squash most frequently available in Mozambique is similar to the giant West Indian or Caribbean variety that can be found in parts of Canada and the U.S. Butternut is another good choice but any winter squash will do. It's the method that's important here.

1-2 lbs. squash, peeled and
  cubed
1 bay leaf
4 or 5 large garlic cloves,
  crushed
1 tblsp. onion, minced
1 tblsp. oil or butter
1 tsp. salt
1/8 tsp. black pepper
1 tsp. fresh ginger, grated
1/4 tsp. curry powder
1/8 tsp. turmeric
1/8 tsp. paprika
1-3 tblsp. lemon juice

Peel, cube and boil the squash in enough water to cover. (If your squash is extremely hard, you may boil it whole or in large chunks until it becomes soft enough to peel and chop.) When the pieces are very soft, lift them out, leaving water in the pot. Mash squash with a fork, or put through a sieve, and return to cooking water. Simmer gently, adding the bay leaf.

Meanwhile, sauté the crushed garlic and the onion in oil or butter. Combine the remaining spices and add them to the butter mixture. Sauté over low heat for 5-10 minutes until flavors have blended well. Then spoon a little of the squash liquid into the skillet with the spice/butter; stir and simmer gently until combined, and pour into the soup pot. Add water to make about 6 cups and stir in lemon juice to taste.

Variations: Chicken stock may be used instead of water, and other vegetables may be added. Among other spices that work well in squash soup are coriander, fennel, celery seed, rosemary and cayenne pepper.

Harira   Morocco
Hearty Soup

Serves 8. Ramadan—the ninth month of the Moslem calendar year—is a time of fasting during daylight hours. Thick, peppery Harira, full of vegetables and legumes, is the traditional Moroccan way of breaking the fast. Each evening at sunset, steamy soup accompanied by dates and honeyed pastries welcomes hungry diners to the table. When making your version, experiment by trying different beans, vegetables and seasonings. Some recipes call for lemon juice to be added during cooking. This one lets individuals squeeze their own at the table.

½ lb. lamb or chicken, diced
2 large onions, chopped
½ cup celery, including leaves, chopped
1 cup parsley, chopped
½ tsp. black pepper, freshly ground
1 tsp. turmeric
1 tsp. ground cinnamon
¼ tsp. ground ginger (optional)
1 tblsp. clarified butter (see recipe, page 9)
½ cup lentils or chickpeas (or both), pre-soaked
2 lbs. tomatoes or 2 tblsp. tomato paste
2 or 3 sprigs of fresh coriander, if available
⅓ cup vermicelli noodles (thin spaghetti)
3 tblsp. unbleached or whole wheat flour
1 lemon, sliced in wedges

In a large, deep pot, combine the meat, onions, celery, parsley, pepper, turmeric, cinnamon, ginger and butter. Stir over medium heat for 15 minutes until ingredients are well browned. Add the lentils or chickpeas along with about 6 cups of water. Stir, partially cover the pot, and simmer for an hour and a half. Purée the tomatoes. (Moroccans would also peel and seed them; see *About peeling* in the Introduction.) Bruise the coriander leaves with a mortar and pestle. Dump them into the pot along with the tomatoes and simmer for another 15-20 minutes. Break vermicelli into inch-long pieces, then bring the mixture to a boil and stir in the noodles. Reduce heat slightly and cook for 2 or 3 minutes.

Meanwhile, dip out about a half cup of the liquid and mix it with the flour to create a smooth paste. Using a wire whisk, quickly stir the flour paste into the soup. Cook for another few minutes until noodles are done, stirring constantly to prevent flour from forming lumps. The texture of the soup should be velvety; if necessary, add more water or more flour (being sure to make a paste before putting flour into the soup). Serve with lemon wedges, which are to be squeezed into each portion at the table.

Variation: Instead of flour, thicken the soup with 2 eggs beaten with a couple of teaspoons of lemon juice. Stir them in just before serving, after removing the pot from the stove.

Snacks and Appetizers

Maacouda With Potatoes   Tunisia

Both Maacouda and Meshwiya (see recipe in this section) are typical Tunisian hors d'oeuvres.

1 lb. potatoes
2 medium onions, finely
    chopped
3-4 oz. parsley, chopped
2 tblsp. butter
½ tsp. salt
¼ tsp. pepper
6 large eggs

Pre-heat the oven to 450°. Peel the potatoes and boil them until very soft; then drain and mash them well. Over low heat, sauté the onions and parsley in butter.

Meanwhile, grease the sides and bottom of a 10-inch round pan. When the onions are transparent, combine onions, parsley, butter, mashed potatoes, salt and pepper. Beat the eggs and stir them in. Pour the mixture into the greased pan and bake for 20 minutes. When slightly cooled, remove from the pan and slice.

Meshwiya   Tunisia

This dish is served as a dip, or spread on small chunks of baguettes. Make it during a season when you can get fresh, vine-ripened tomatoes.

3-4 tomatoes
1 green bell pepper
1 tsp. salt
1 tblsp. cumin
2 cloves garlic, crushed
2 tsp. lemon juice
1/4-1/2 cup olive oil, to taste

Traditionally, the tomato and pepper skins are removed by grilling over an open flame. If you want to peel your vegetables, dip them into boiling water for a minute or so, and follow with a plunge into cold water. The skins should slip off fairly easily. Chop the peeled tomatoes and pepper into small chunks.

Add the salt, cumin and crushed garlic. If not eating immediately, store the mixture, covered, in the refrigerator. Before serving, add lemon juice and oil.

Variations: Other common additions to Meshwiya are chunks of tuna, bits of black olive, and chopped, hard-boiled eggs.

Kulikuli   Nigeria
Peanut Balls

1 lb. roasted peanuts
1/4-1/2 cup peanut oil
1 small onion, finely chopped
1 tsp. cayenne pepper
1 tsp. salt
oil for frying

Grind or pound nuts, or put through a blender or food processor, adding just enough oil to make a smooth paste. With wet hands, squeeze the nut mixture to remove excess oil. Sauté the onions, cayenne and salt in a tablespoon of oil until golden, then knead into the peanut paste. Shape the mixture into 1-inch diameter balls, adding a few drops of water if necessary to make them hold together. Drop the balls into hot oil (see *About frying* in the Introduction), or flatten and fry in a skillet. Cook for 2-3 minutes until the outsides are crisp.

Akara   # Nigeria
Black-eyed Pea Balls

Serves 4

1 cup dried black-eyed peas
1 egg
½ of a small onion, finely
    chopped
½ tsp. chili pepper, chopped or
    ¼ tsp. cayenne
1 tsp. salt
vegetable oil for frying

Soak the peas in cool water for 10-20 minutes. Then, with your hands in the water, rub peas between your palms to remove the skins, which will float to the top. Skim them off and repeat the cleaning process until there are no more skins. Drain the peas and purée them in a blender or food processor with about ⅓ cup water. (It's best to blend the peas in two or three batches so as not to clog the machine.) If the mixture appears dry rather than pasty, add more water, a few teaspoons at a time. To the last portion of the peas, add the egg, onions, pepper and salt.

Combine all the batches in a deep bowl and mix thoroughly with a flat wooden spoon. Beat for 2 or 3 minutes until the paste is light and airy. It should be of a consistency that can hold its shape in a spoon and roll off slowly. Drop by heaping tablespoons into 375° oil, frying until golden brown. (You may use either deep fat or a couple of inches of oil in a large, heavy skillet.) If you don't have a candy thermometer, test oil temperature by dropping in one ball. It should sputter upon contact and become golden brown, without scorching, in about 5 minutes. As the balls are fried—3 or 4 at a time is all most pots can accomodate—remove with a slotted spoon and drain on clean, absorbent cloths.

Dabo Kolo   Ethiopia
Crunchy Spice Bites

Makes about 4 cups. These tangy tidbits can be served as you would popcorn or peanuts.

2 cups unbleached or whole
   wheat flour
2 tblsp. berbere (see recipes,
   pages 3 and 4) or cayenne
   pepper
1 tblsp. sugar
1½ tsp. salt
¼ cup light oil

Pre-heat oven to 350°. In a bowl, combine flour, berbere or pepper, sugar and salt. Gradually mix in about ⅔ cup water until a thick paste forms. Dump the mixture onto a floured board and knead it until you have a stiff dough. Make a well in the center of the dough ball and pour in the oil; fold dough over the oil and knead again until well mixed, about 5 minutes.

Cover the dough with a cloth to keep it moist, and break off chunks of it to roll into ¼-inch round strips. Cut the strips into ½-inch long pieces, preferably using scissors so that the ends will be pinched. Bake on a flat sheet or in baking tins for 20-30 minutes, until crisp. Stir three or four times to ensure even browning. When cool, store in airtight container.

Yeshimbra Asa

Pea Flour Fish

Ethiopia

The Ethiopian Coptic church still uses the ancient sign of the fish as a symbol for Christianity. These chickpea flour fish are traditional during Lent, when fasting rules require that no meat or dairy products be eaten. Flour made from chickpeas can be found at many natural food or ethnic groceries.

½ cup onions or shallots, finely
  chopped
2 tblsp. cayenne pepper
½ tsp. salt
⅓ cup oil
⅓ cup berbere (see recipes,
  pages 3 and 4)
2 cups chickpea flour
oil for frying

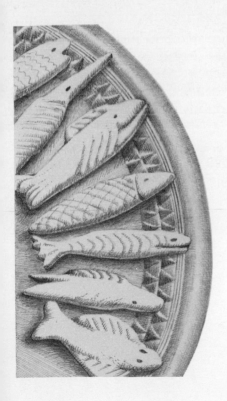

In a dry, heavy pot, stir the onions over low heat until browned. Add ⅓ cup water along with the cayenne, salt and oil. Simmer for 5-10 minutes before adding another ⅔ cup water and the berbere. Bring to a boil, cover, and reduce heat, stirring occasionally. (This mixture will serve as both a cooking medium and a sauce.)

Meanwhile, add just enough water to the pea flour to make a thick dough, similar to that for rolled cookies. Try using ½ cup water, though you may find you need another ¼ cup or so, a teaspoon at a time, until the mixture adheres to itself to form a ball. Roll the dough out on a lightly floured surface to a thickness of about ¼ inch, and cut into shapes with cookie cutters or a sharp knife. Ethiopians make fish shapes and decorate them with all sorts of designs.

Fry the pieces in moderately hot oil in a heavy skillet for 3-4 minutes, turning several times. When they are crisp and brown, cautiously spoon them into the sauce in the pot. Simmer gently for 5 or 6 minutes, being careful not to break the shapes. Lift pieces out with a slotted spoon, drain on clean cloths and serve with the sauce.

Sautéed Almonds   Morocco

Makes about 5 cups. These crisp, crunchy nuts are nourishing snacks; bottled in a nice jar, they are unusual, handsome gifts. For the best buy, purchase almonds unpeeled in bulk at a specialty store.

2 lb. shelled almonds
2 tblsp. salt
1 cup vegetable oil

Peel the almonds by pouring them gradually into gently boiling water, until you have about a cup in the pot. After a minute or two, lift the first batch out with a slotted spoon, and replace with another cupful. (Although the water will be tinted a brownish-purple, you don't need to change it.) When cool enough to handle, pinch one end of the skin on each nut, and the skinned almond will pop out the other side. (This is a popular activity among children, because there are sure to be at least a few nuts flying across the room!) To speed the process, the boiled nuts can be cooled by dumping them in ice water for a couple of minutes.

Mix skinned almonds with the salt and let stand 15 minutes. Meanwhile, heat oil in a large, heavy skillet until a test almond sputters gently. If it pops furiously the oil is too hot, and if it just sits there the oil is too cool. Sauté the almonds in two or three groups, depending on the size of your skillet, stirring frequently to prevent scorching. They will gradually become a rich, golden brown.

After 20-30 minutes, when all the nuts in the pan are browned, remove with a slotted spoon and drain on a soft, lint-free cloth. (Paper towels may be used, but we prefer old linen towels that can be pressed into service again and again.) When cool, store in an airtight container.

28

Hot Plantain Crisps   Ghana

Many supermarkets now carry plantains alongside bananas in the produce section. If yours doesn't, look in an ethnic or specialty grocery.

4 plantains
4 tsp. lemon juice
4 tsp. ground ginger
4 tsp. cayenne pepper
oil for frying

Slice the plantains into rounds ¼-inch thick, and sprinkle lemon juice over the pieces, stirring to moisten. In a separate bowl, combine the ginger and pepper. Heat about ¼ inch of oil in a heavy skillet until a test piece of plantain sputters. Roll plantain pieces a few at a time in the spice mixture to coat surfaces, then transfer to the skillet. Fry until outsides are crisp and golden. With a slotted spoon, remove plantain to an absorbent cloth for cooling. Serve hot.

Dithotse   Lesotho
Roasted Melon Seeds

In traditional southern African societies, pieces of pumpkin and melon were dried in the sun for winter use. When soaked and cooked, they provided important nutrients during the long months of cold weather. Their roasted seeds were eaten either hot or cold. Try these as a party or after-school snack.

1 cup seeds from a fresh melon
   or pumpkin
2 tsp. salt

Wash the seeds well, rubbing to remove any pulp. Stir salt into the wet seeds. Heat on the stove a dry empty pot or large skillet—preferably cast iron. Add the salted seeds. Cook for 6 or 8 minutes over moderate heat, stirring continuously. Seeds are ready when they have cracked open. They are meant to be savored one at a time, rather than in handfuls.

29

Samoosas

Southern Africa

Savory filled pastries of Indian origin are an everyday food in much of southern Africa and are a common feature of east African cuisine as well. Although they are excellent party food, several of them can make a meal. Choose either meat or vegetable fillings, and make your own pastry or use purchased egg roll dough. Although this recipe is lengthy because the descriptions are somewhat complex, samoosas are not difficult to prepare. Amounts given here make about 2 dozen.

For meat filling:

2 tsp. fresh ginger, grated or 1 tsp. ground ginger
3 small cloves garlic
1 lb. ground lamb or ground beef
2 large onions, thinly sliced
1 tblsp. ghurum masala (see recipe, page 6)
1 tblsp. curry powder (see recipes, pages 5 and 6)
1 tsp. salt
oil, if needed

Crush ginger and garlic with a mortar and pestle. Combine all ingredients in a large skillet and simmer for 30 minutes, stirring frequently. Add a bit of oil if meat is too lean to grease the pan. When meat is well browned, drain off any excess fat. Set aside.

For vegetable filling:

3 medium potatoes
2 carrots
1 cup fresh green peas or 1 8-oz. package frozen peas
2-3 tblsp. oil or clarified butter
1 cup onions, finely chopped
2 tsp. fresh ginger, grated or ½ tsp. ground ginger
2 large cloves garlic, crushed
½ tsp. coriander seeds, crushed
2 tblsp. fresh coriander, finely chopped (optional)
2 tsp. lemon juice

Peel potatoes or don't, as you wish. Boil potatoes and carrots until both are soft but still firm. Cut into small cubes about ½-inch square. In a separate pot, cook peas just until tender. Meanwhile, heat oil or butter until a test onion sputters upon contact with it. Add onions, ginger, garlic and coriander and saute 6 or 8 minutes, stirring constantly. Mix in the lemon juice and the cooked vegetables, gently adding peas last. Heat through, then set aside.

For pastry:

2 cups unbleached flour
¾ tsp. salt
1½ tblsp. oil or clarified butter
    (see recipe, page 9)
½-¾ cup water

Sift flour and salt together. Make a well in the center of the mixture and quickly pour in oil and water. Stir briskly until combined, gradually adding more water if necessary. You should aim for a slightly moist dough that sticks together. On a lightly floured surface, knead dough for 10 minutes until smooth and elastic. Cover with a damp towel.

To assemble samoosas, break off pieces of dough (leaving what's left under the towel) and shape into balls. Roll each ball into a circle about ¹⁄₁₆ of an inch thick and 5 inches across. Cut the circle in half. On one side of one half-circle, put a heaping tablespoon of filling. Fold the other side of the same half-circle over the filling to make a triangle. Seal by brushing a bit of water along the edges and pinching them together with your fingers. Repeat with the other half-circle, and continue in the same fashion until all the dough and filling are used.

Deep-fat fry the samoosas (see *About frying* in the Introduction), or heat 2 inches of oil in a large skillet to a temperature of 375°. Fry each samoosa until golden brown and crisp on each side. Drain on a clean, absorbent cloth or on paper towels.

See next page for pastry variation.

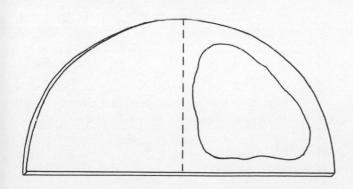
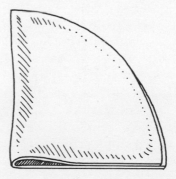

Variation: Buy a pound of spring roll or egg roll pastry. Separate the pieces, which will be about 6 inches square, and cut each one in half so that you have pieces that are about 6 inches long and 3 inches wide. To make the samoosas, imagine the top 3 inches as a square that you will fold in half along its diagonal. But first, on the lower corner of the square, put a spoonful of filling. Fold top half down over the filling diagonally, so that the top of your strip is now a triangle. Then fold this triangle over the next section of the strip so that you have a square. Finally, fold once again along the diagonal so that you end with a multi-layered triangle. Seal the edges and cook as described in the pastry instructions.

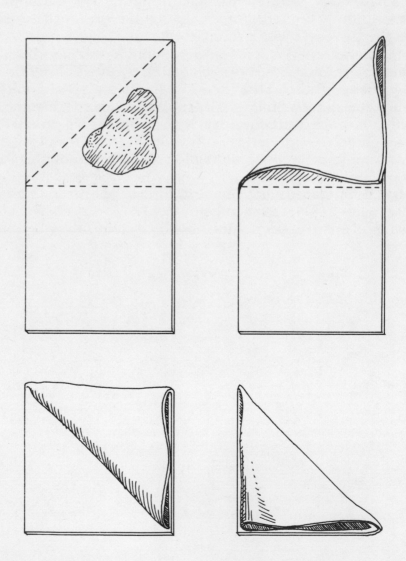

Karringmelkbeskuit　　　South Africa
Buttermilk Rusks

Makes about 2 dozen, depending on size. These classic rusks are for dipping into milk or coffee at snacktime.

3 cups unbleached flour
2 cups whole wheat flour
½ cup sugar
1 tblsp. baking powder
½ lb. (2 sticks) butter
1 egg, beaten
1-2 cups buttermilk

Preheat oven to 350°. Combine flours with sugar and baking powder. Grate the butter and quickly blend it in with your fingertips. (The texture should be gritty.) Stir in the egg, followed by a cup of the buttermilk. Continue to add milk a few spoonsful at a time, until batter has the consistency of biscuit dough—thick and just moist enough to adhere to itself.

With floured hands, pinch off golf-ball size pieces of the dough. Roll into balls and place on a greased baking sheet. Bake for 20 minutes, or until a cake tester inserted into the dough comes out clean. The surfaces should be golden brown.

Let the oven cool to 200°. Pile the cooked pieces into baking dishes or onto cookie sheets. Leave in the oven overnight to dry. The next morning, let the rusks cool and then store them in an airtight container.

Chicken

In much of Africa, as in the southern United States, chicken is a special-occasion dish. When available, it is also used for family meals, though normally in less quantity than called for by the recipes here. The popularity of one-pot dinners is partly due to the way they stretch a limited amount of food among many people. The couscous and tagines of north Africa, the wats of the Horn, the groundnut stews of the west coast and the curries of the east and south are all variations on a theme—spiced meat and vegetables served with filling grains: bread, rice, or stiff porridge.

If you haven't pre-soaked the legumes you'll need for some of these dishes, don't despair: consult the tips on cutting cooking time in *About grains* in the Introduction.

The consistency of most of the dishes can vary according to your taste. A thick sauce may be thinned by the addition of water and a thin one can be thickened by "reducing"—evaporating the water by bubbling the sauce over moderate heat. But check frequently, and stir occasionally, to prevent burning and sticking.

African chicken recipes call for whole birds—because that, of course, is how chickens come. But you may prepare these dishes with your choice of parts. To reduce fat, we generally remove the chicken skin from all pieces except wings and backs.

The Moroccan tagines (or, more properly in the plural, *twaugin*) generally are eaten only with freshly-baked bread. We've found them also delicious over rice.

A number of these dishes need fresh coriander (although you can do without it if you must). Look for it in Latin or Asian markets, where it will be called *cilantro* or *Chinese parsley*.

Stews, Plain and Fancy

Couscous   Algeria

Serves 4-6. This Algerian version of couscous with chicken is relatively simple to prepare.

1 chicken, cut into pieces
¼ cup olive oil
2 tblsp. clarified butter (see
　recipe, page 9)
1 onion, sliced in rounds
1 large ripe tomato
½ tsp. ground black pepper
1 cinnamon stick
½ tsp. salt
¼ cup dry chickpeas, soaked
　overnight
couscous (see couscous section
　in *Grains and Bread* chapter).

Unless you are using a couscousière, combine chicken, oil, butter, onion, tomato, pepper, cinnamon stick, and salt in a large, heavy pot. Stir over medium heat to coat and brown the chicken. After about 5 minutes, cover with 1½ cups water and bring to a boil. Toss in the chickpeas, then simmer, covered, 30-40 minutes until chicken is tender. Remove the chicken pieces and set them aside.

Continue to cook the mixture in the pot until chickpeas are tender, perhaps another 1½ hours. Add more water, if necessary, to retain roughly the same level. When chickpeas are done, return the chicken to the pot to heat through. To serve in a traditional manner, distribute the couscous in a large bowl or platter with curved edges, and ladle on as much liquid from the stew as the couscous will absorb. Pile chicken in the center, and finish by ladling chickpeas and sauce over all.

Djedj b'l-qasbour
Coriander Chicken

Algeria

Serves 4-6

1 chicken (fryer), cut into pieces
1 tblsp. butter
4 tblsp. oil
4 large cloves of garlic
1 tsp. turmeric or saffron
salt and pepper to taste
sprig of fresh coriander leaves,
    or 2 tsp. ground coriander
¼ lb. purple olives, pitted (Greek
    or Italian rather than the
    "ripe" American type)
1 lemon, sliced

Brown the chicken in butter and oil in a large, heavy skillet over moderate heat. Add the garlic cloves, spices, and coriander (chopped fine). Cook for about ten minutes, turning the chicken pieces occasionally to distribute sauce evenly. Stir in enough water to cover, about 1 cup, and simmer over low heat, adding more water if necessary until the chicken is tender. Add olives and lemon and cook over somewhat higher heat for 8-10 more minutes, or until sauce is reduced. Serve over rice or couscous.

Chicken Tagine
with Chickpeas and Beans

Morocco

Serves 4-6

1 large stewing chicken
2 tblsp. butter
5 medium onions, chopped
1 tsp. salt (optional)
1 tsp. turmeric or saffron
1 tsp. cinnamon
⅓ cup dry chickpeas
    (pre-soaked)
⅓ cup dry broad beans
    (pre-soaked)
⅓ cup peeled almonds (see
    About peeling in the
    Introduction)
1 small bunch parsley, chopped
juice of 1 lemon
1 tomato, chopped

In a pot that has a tight-fitting lid, braise the chicken and one of the onions in butter. Cover with water, about 2 cups. Add the salt, turmeric or saffron, and cinnamon, then bring to a boil. Reduce heat to low, put in peas and beans, and cook slowly for one hour or until the legumes are done. Stir occasionally, adding more water if needed. When the legumes are soft, add the rest of the onions, the almonds, and all but a few of the parsley leaves. Simmer slowly until onions are cooked, about 20-30 minutes. Just before serving, sprinkle with lemon juice, remaining parsley, and the chopped tomato.

M'qualli   Morocco
Chicken Tagine with Lemons

Serves 8-10

2 chickens (3-4 lbs. each), whole
   or cut into pieces
1-2 tsp. salt
¼ cup olive oil
4 tblsp. clarified butter (see
   recipe, page 9)
2 tsp. fresh ginger, grated, or 1
   tsp. ground ginger
1 whole onion
3 cloves garlic, crushed
1 tsp. turmeric or saffron
10 small olives (choose green or
   black, but use Greek, Italian,
   or Spanish, not the bland
   American style intended for
   munching)
peel of 1 lemon, cut into strips

Place chickens in a pot with all the other ingredients except olives and lemon peel. Cover with water and bring to a boil, turning the chickens over to make sure they are well-coated with sauce. Cook over moderate heat, covered, adding a little water if necessary, and basting the chickens with sauce from time to time. Remove the onion as soon as it is cooked.

When chickens are done, add the olives and lemon peel, and let simmer slowly a few minutes longer. To serve, place the chickens on a serving platter, top with olives and lemon rinds, and pour sauce over the whole dish.

Chicken Tagine
with Olive and Pickled Lemons   Morocco

Serves 4-6. You must plan this dish far enough ahead to have the pickled lemons ready.

1 2-lb. stewing chicken
½ tsp. salt
1 tsp. fresh ginger, grated
1 clove garlic, crushed
4 tblsp. olive oil
¼ tsp. saffron
1 tblsp. butter
10 olives
1 or 2 pickled lemons (see
   recipe, page 10)

Salt the chicken and put it in a covered stewing pan, together with all the other ingredients except the olives and pickled lemons. Add about 1½ cups water and cook over moderate heat, turning the chicken from time to time to baste it with the sauce. When chicken is tender, add the lemons and olives. Cook slowly for another 10-15 minutes, stirring occasionally. When served, the sauce should be rather thick.

Chicken Tagine
with Prunes and Honey

Morocco

Serves 8-10. This elegant dish always gets an enthusiastic reception and is a good choice for serving guests.

2 chickens (3-4 lbs. each), cut
   into pieces
2-4 tsp. salt (optional)
1 tsp. pepper
½ tsp. saffron or turmeric
2 sticks cinnamon
2 large onions, finely chopped
2 sticks butter (may be reduced
   or combined with oil)
1 lb. prunes, washed and pitted
2 tsp. ground cinnamon
4 tblsp. honey
½ lb. almonds, without skins
   (see *About peeling* in the
   Introduction)
2 tblsp. vegetable or peanut oil
1 tblsp. sesame seeds

Place the chicken, salt, pepper, turmeric or saffron, cinnamon sticks, onions and butter in a large, heavy pot. Add water to cover, about 2 cups, and bring to a boil. Cover the pot, reduce the heat, and simmer until the chicken is done, adding water if necessary. Remove and set aside the chicken pieces.

Stir prunes into the simmering liquid. After 15 minutes, add ground cinnamon and honey, and cook until the sauce itself has a honey-like consistency. (Depending on your pot, your stove, and the moisture in your chicken, this can take from 15 minutes to more than an hour.)

When the sauce seems almost ready, lightly sauté almonds in oil in a heavy skillet. Remove the almonds with a slotted spoon and set aside. Pour off all but a thin coating of the oil and carefully toast the sesame seeds, stirring constantly to prevent scorching. Return chicken to the sauce for a quick re-heating, then place it in a serving dish. Top with the sauce, almonds, and sesame seeds.

Doro Wat
Chicken Stew

Ethiopia

Serves 8-10. If you haven't tasted Ethiopian food, you'll be surprised at the unique flavor of Doro Wat. Even if you have a chance to sample it at one of the growing number of Ethiopian restaurants in large cities, it's a dish worth trying at home. To eat it the Ethiopian way, pass around a tray of injera, and place a large platter of wat in the center of the table so that everyone can reach it. Tear off pieces of injera with your right hand. Fold the bread around bits of stew and eat, without touching your fingers to either the stew or to your mouth (a trick that requires practice!)

2 3-lb. chickens, cut into pieces
3 sticks butter
3 lbs. onion, finely chopped
2 large cloves garlic, minced, or
  2 tsp. garlic powder
3 heaping tblsp. berbere (see
  recipes, pages 3 and 4)
9 oz. tomato paste
10 hard-boiled eggs, slightly
  scored
1 tsp. ground black pepper
injera (see recipe in *Grains and
  Bread* chapter)

Remove skin from the chicken and score each piece slightly with a knife so the sauce can penetrate.

In a large stew pot, melt the butter, then sauté the onions and garlic for five minutes. Add berbere, followed by tomato paste, stirring occasionally while the mixture simmers for about 15 minutes. A piece at a time, stir in the chicken, coating well with the sauce.

Continue to simmer, adding enough water to maintain the consistency of a thick soup. When chicken is half done, after about 20 minutes, put in the hard-boiled eggs. Cover and continue cooking until chicken is tender. The dish is ready when oil has risen to the top. Add black pepper and let sit until slightly cooled.

Serve with injera.

Groundnut Stew

Stew made from groundnuts, or what folks in the U.S. call peanuts, is among those foods that make guests exclaim in delight. Although early English settlers learned to like it—it's still on the menu at inns in the colonial Williamsburg restoration—the stew fell into obscurity at some later time. These recipes will persuade you that it's worth rediscovering.

Although the west African versions are probably best known outside Africa, the use of peanuts as a soup or stew base and as a sauce is widespread on the continent, as these recipes from as far apart as Ghana and Uganda illustrate.

Use the kind of pure peanut butter—without sugar, please—found in natural food stores, or make your own by grinding peanuts in a blender or food processor, using a small amount of peanut oil if necessary to achieve a creamy texture. When adding peanut butter to the stew, first mix it well with about half a cup of hot broth from the pot. To serve, let individuals ladle the finished stew over plates of rice or stiff porridge. (See *fufu* and other porridge recipes in the *Grains and Bread* chapter. Also see recipe for groundnut soup in *Soups, Snacks and Appetizers*.)

Chickennat   Uganda

Serves 4-6

1 2-3 lb. chicken, cut into pieces
1 tsp. salt
½ tsp. ground black pepper
½ cup butter
½ cup onions, chopped
1 pint chicken stock
¾ cup pure peanut butter, or 1
   lb. roasted peanuts, ground to
   a paste
1-2 egg yolks
several sprigs of parsley, coarsely
   chopped

Rub the chicken pieces with salt and pepper. Melt butter in a large, heavy skillet or stew pot, and add the chicken and onions. Cover and simmer over lowest heat, periodically adding stock until you have used it all. (If you don't have stock, add plain water or bouillon). After 15 minutes, remove half a cup of the cooking liquid to thin the peanut butter or paste. Add to the pot and bring to a boil. Reduce heat and then whisk some of the hot stew liquid into the egg yolks. Add to the pot and stir to incorporate the egg mixture into the stew. Simmer gently until chicken is done. Be careful not to heat the stew above a simmer from this point. Garnish with parsley leaves and serve with rice or a corn porridge.

Groundnut Stew   West Africa

Serves 4-6

¼-⅓ cup peanut or other frying
  oil
3-lb. chicken, cut into pieces
2 medium onions, sliced ¼ inch
  thick
¾ cup peanut butter
6 cups tomatoes, chopped
1-inch piece of fresh ginger
1 tsp. salt
½ tsp. black pepper
1 tsp. cayenne pepper
2 cups okra (optional)

Heat the oil in a large, heavy skillet. When it is moderately hot, sauté the chicken parts until just golden brown, and remove them to a large stew pot. In the skillet, sauté onion slices until slightly limp, then pile them onto the chicken. Cover the mixture with about 2 cups of water and bring to a boil. Thin the peanut butter with a bit of the broth and add it to the pot along with the tomatoes, ginger, salt, peppers, and okra. (Okra will aid the thickening.) Reduce heat and simmer for 30-45 minutes until chicken is tender. Remove the ginger piece before serving.

Hkatenkwan   Ghana

Serves 4-6

3-lb. chicken, cut into pieces
2 tsp. grated fresh ginger, or 1
  tsp. ground ginger
½ of a whole onion
2 tblsp. tomato paste
1 tblsp. peanut oil, or other light
  cooking oil
1 cup onion, well chopped
1 cup tomatoes, chopped
⅔ cup peanut butter
2 tsp. salt
2 hot chilies, crushed, or 1 tsp.
  cayenne powder
1 medium-size eggplant,
  peeled and cubed
2 cups fresh or frozen okra

Boil chicken with ginger and the onion half, using about 2 cups water. Meanwhile, in a separate large pot, fry tomato paste in the oil over low heat for about 5 minutes. Add to the paste the chopped onions and tomatoes, stirring occasionally until the onions are clear. Remove the partially-cooked chicken pieces and put them, along with about half the broth, in the large pot. Add the peanut butter, salt and peppers. Cook for 5 minutes before stirring in the eggplant and okra. Continue cooking until chicken and vegetables are tender. Add more broth as needed to maintain a thick, stewy consistency.

Mafé   Senegal

Chicken Peanut Stew

Serves 8-10. The version of groundnut stew called "mafé" has its origins among the Bambara people of Mali. But Monique Biarnès writes that mafé is so well integrated into the cookery of neighboring Senegal that it is considered one of that country's culinary pillars.

2 chickens, cut into pieces
¾ cup peanut oil
2 large onions, chopped
2-3 tomatoes
¼ cup tomato paste
1 tsp. salt
1 cup peanut butter
1 small cabbage, chopped
3 sweet potatoes, cut into
   chunks
6 carrots
6 turnips
12 okra
1 chili pepper, or ½ tsp. cayenne
   pepper

Brown chicken in hot oil in a large, heavy pot. Add half the onion and stir until golden brown. Peel tomatoes if you wish (see *About peeling* in the Introduction), then chop them into chunks. Thin tomato paste with about half a cup of water, and add tomatoes and paste to the pot.

Boil 4 cups of water, and pour that into the pot as well, along with the salt. While the mixture boils gently, thin peanut butter with some of the hot pot liquid and stir it in gradually. Reduce heat and simmer for half an hour. Then begin adding the vegetables, letting each simmer for 5 minutes or so before putting in the next one. Cook until chicken and all the vegetables are tender.

Meanwhile, crush or grind the second onion with the pepper. Add during the last 10 minutes of cooking.

Dovi   Zimbabwe
Peanut Butter Stew
Serves 4-6

2 medium onions, finely
  chopped
2 tblsp. butter
2 cloves garlic, finely sliced and
  crushed
1 tsp. salt
½ tsp. pepper
1 chili pepper or ½ tsp. cayenne
  pepper
2 green bell peppers, chopped
1 chicken, cut into pieces
3-4 fresh or canned tomatoes
6 tblsp. smooth peanut butter
½ lb. spinach or pumpkin leaves

In a large stew pot over moderate heat, sauté onions in butter until golden brown. Add garlic, salt, and hot peppers. Stir for 2 or 3 minutes, then add green peppers and chicken. When all the chicken pieces are brown on every side, mash tomatoes with a fork and mix them into the stew, along with about 2 cups of water. Reduce heat and simmer for 5-10 minutes.

Thin the peanut butter with a few spoons of hot broth and add half the resulting paste to the pot. Simmer until meat is well cooked. Meanwhile, boil spinach or pumpkin leaves for several minutes until tender. Drain, and toss with the remainder of the peanut butter paste. Serve stew and greens together.

Curries

Southern African curries are a blend of Malay and Indian influences. To a greater extent than the Asian dishes of east Africa, they have become *indigenized*—a commonplace part of many people's diets.

Serious cooks say that all good curries begin with onions fried gently in a combination of ghee (clarified butter) and light vegetable oil. Sliced fine, the onions are cooked only until they turn golden. Meanwhile, the vegetables and the meat, if any, are combined with various spices to soak up flavor before being added to the pot. In Indian dishes, tomato skins are considered offensive, but when cooking for ourselves, we leave ours unpeeled, as we do potatoes (except the crisply-fried ones in biryani).

These recipes, more than most, rely on freshly pounded spices. You will notice that there is no curry powder in the ingredients, because authentic curries are made with different spice blends, depending on the type of food being prepared. However, if you're pressed for time, or can't find the whole spices you need, look for a potent curry powder in a specialty food store (even Indian shops carry curry powder these days, though you're not likely to see an Indian buying it!). The hot *Madras* kind is among the most popular. You also can make your own with the help of the recipes on pages 5 and 6. Use the powder, to taste, as a substitute for the spices called for in the recipe. However, if you use a purchased curry powder you should still add cardamom, cloves and cinnamon as the recipe directs, since those aromatics are not a part of most commercial preparations.

By American standards, traditional curries of Asian origin are very hot. The amounts of pepper given here would be considered quite mild, so if you're daring, or accustomed to hot foods, you may want to double or triple the pepper right away. Otherwise, taste first, then add more at the table if you like.

Curries are served with long-grained rice—*Basmati* is a good choice—or with such Indian breads as *chapati* and *roti*. Other common accompaniments are yogurt and cucumber salads, and chutneys. Many people like to serve additional condiments including finely-diced onions, nuts, sliced bananas, grated coconut, and raisins.

Kurma   Southern Africa
Quick Chicken Curry

1 chicken, cut into pieces
3 tblsp. clarified butter (see
   recipe, page 9) or oil
1 large onion, sliced
1-inch piece of fresh ginger,
   grated, or 1 tsp. ground ginger
3 medium cloves garlic, sliced or
   slivered
1 tsp. salt
1 stick cinnamon
2 cardamom pods
2 cloves
2 whole peppercorns
2 small chili peppers or 1 tsp.
   cayenne pepper

Wash the chicken and pat dry. In a large stew pot, combine all the ingredients. Cook, stirring constantly, until steaming. Reduce the heat, add about 1 cup water, cover, and simmer until chicken is done.

Kalya e Khaas
Traditional Chicken Curry

Southern Africa

Serves 4-6

2-3 lbs. chicken pieces
1 cup yogurt
1 cup tomato, chopped
1 stick cinnamon, or ½ tsp.
   ground cinnamon
3 cardamom pods, slightly
   crushed, or 1 tsp. ground
   cardamom
2-4 whole cloves
3 whole black peppercorns
½ tsp. cumin seeds, or ¼ tsp.
   ground cumin
3-4 whole green chilies
½ tsp. saffron powder (optional)
¼ tsp. turmeric
1 tsp. cayenne pepper
1 tsp. fresh ginger, grated
1 tsp. garlic, grated
1 tsp. salt
2 medium-size onions, finely
   sliced
¼ cup clarified butter (see
   recipe, page 9)
¼ cup oil
sprig of fresh coriander leaves
sprig of fresh mint leaves

Wash the chicken and pat dry. Combine the yogurt, tomatoes, cinnamon, cardamom, cloves, peppercorns, cumin, chilies, saffron, turmeric, cayenne, ginger, garlic and salt. Pour mixture over the chicken, turning the pieces until they are well-coated. While they marinate, fry the onions gently in the butter and oil until light, golden brown. You may use either a large, heavy skillet or a stew pot.

Remove the onions. When they have cooled slightly, crush them with the back of a spoon. Return them to the pot or skillet, along with the entire contents of the marinating bowl. Simmer until chicken is tender, adding small amounts of water as necessary to keep contents from sticking. Garnish with fresh coriander and mint leaves, and serve with rice or Indian bread.

Variation: In the last 10-15 minutes of cooking, toss in a handful of whole, pitted prunes and/or a dozen whole, peeled almonds. (See *About peeling* in the Introduction.) You may also add potatoes. If you do, chop them into pieces about 3 inches across, and boil them in water until soft but still firm. Sauté in oil to crisp the surfaces before adding them to curry in the last few minutes before serving.

Murghi Kalya
Chicken Curry Variation

Serves 4-6

Southern Africa

1 2-lb. chicken, cut into pieces
1 tsp. hot chili peppers
1 2-inch square piece of fresh
  coconut, grated, or 3 tblsp.
  packaged coconut
  (unsweetened)
1 tsp. cayenne pepper
¼ tsp. saffron powder or
  turmeric
1 tsp. garlic, crushed
1 tsp. ginger, grated and
  crushed, or ½ tsp. ground
  ginger
1 tsp. salt
¼ cup ghee or butter
¼ cup oil
2 medium-size onions, chopped
1 cup yogurt
juice of ½ lemon
1 lime, sliced
¼ cup slivered almonds

Wash the chicken and drain in a colander. Set aside. Using a mortar and pestle or 2 stones, grind or pound together the peppers, coconut and almonds. Add to this mixture the cayenne pepper, saffron or turmeric, garlic, ginger and salt. In the butter and oil, gently fry the onions just until golden brown. Remove them to cool (saving the butter/oil) and crush with the back of a spoon. In a bowl, combine the chicken, spice mixture, and onions with the yogurt and lemon juice. Marinate for 30-45 minutes before turning the entire contents of the bowl into a large baking dish. Pour the butter/oil over the mixture, and lay the lime slices across the top. Cover with a lid or foil and bake in a 350° oven for one hour, or until chicken is cooked. For the last ten minutes, uncover and sprinkle the almonds across the top.

Serva Curry
Gravy Curry

Southern Africa

Serves 6-8

2 lbs. chicken pieces
3 large onions, finely sliced
¼ cup clarified butter (see
   recipe, page 9)
¼ cup oil
1 tsp. fresh ginger, grated and
   crushed, or ½ tsp. ground
   ginger
1 tsp. garlic, crushed
1 tsp. salt
1 tsp. turmeric
1 tsp. fresh coriander leaves or
   ½ tsp. ground coriander
1 tsp. whole cumin seeds,
   pounded, or 1 tsp. ground
   cumin
2 tsp. fresh chili pepper,
   pounded, or 1 tsp. cayenne
   pepper
3 cardamom pods
1 stick cinnamon
3-4 whole cloves
3-4 peppercorns
1 medium eggplant, peeled and
   diced
4 medium tomatoes, chopped
   and somewhat crushed
5 large potatoes, halved or
   quartered
1 tsp. ghurum masala (see
   recipe, page 6)
2 tblsp. shallots or spring
   onions, minced (optional)

Wash the chicken pieces and drain in a colander. Meanwhile, fry half the onions in the butter and oil until golden. Add the chicken, the remaining onions, all the spices, the eggplant, and 1 cup water, mixing well. Simmer for 10 minutes before adding the tomatoes, and for another 15 minutes before adding the potatoes along with 2 more cups of water. Cook until the chicken and potatoes are done. Just before serving, stir in the ghurum masala and shallots.

Quick Fruit Curry   South Africa

One of the exceptions to the general rule, this provocative but simple dish does use curry powder. Infinite variations are possible, using whatever fresh or dried fruits you have available. Although an adaptation of a "true" curry, it has an easy, pleasant flavor that most people like.

1 chicken, cut into pieces
2 tblsp. oil
1 tblsp. butter
1 small onion, chopped
3 heaping tblsp. curry powder
½ cup fresh apples, diced
½ cup dried apricots, chopped
½ cup raisins
1 tsp. salt
3 tblsp. vinegar or fresh lemon
   juice
¼ cup peanuts, slightly crushed

Brown the chicken in oil and butter over moderate heat. Remove pieces and set aside. Lightly sauté the onions in the same large skillet or pot. Stir in the curry powder, return chicken to the pot, and cook for 3-5 minutes, turning pieces several times. Add the fruits, salt, vinegar and peanuts, with enough water to cover. Bring to a boil, reduce heat, cover and simmer until chicken is tender, about 45 minutes. If the sauce is too thin to ladle well over rice, cook uncovered another 15-20 minutes until liquid is reduced.

Jollof Rice   Gambia

Serves 6-8. A kind of west African paella, Jollof Rice makes an excellent buffet dish for parties. You can put in as many kinds of meat as you like or can afford—or no meat at all. Shrimp makes an extravagant but wonderful addition. Use a heavy pot or large cast iron skillet to discourage burning; stirring often is the key to success. A large wooden spoon works well as an implement. Whatever pot you use, you'll need to be able to cover it tightly. If you don't have a lid, try using an oven-proof plate or platter.

1-2 chickens, chopped into small
   pieces
oil for frying
6 medium onions, chopped
4 green bell peppers, chopped
¼-½ lb. shrimp
¾ cup carrots, chopped
¾ cup stringbeans, broken into
   pieces
¾ cup peas
6 tomatoes, chopped
1 tsp. salt
½ tsp. pepper
1-2 tsp. cayenne pepper
sprig of thyme, crushed, or 1
   tsp. dried thyme
3-4 cups rice
¼-½ cup tomato paste

In a heavy pot large enough to hold everything, brown the chicken in oil. Add onions and peppers and cook over medium heat for 5-10 minutes.

Meanwhile, in a separate skillet, sauté the shrimp in a small amount of oil and pre-cook the carrots, beans and peas—or other vegetables of your choice—until about half done, 5 minutes or so. (You may boil them all together if you like.) Drain the vegetables and add, along with the shrimp, to the chicken pot. Reduce heat to low and simmer for 5 minutes.

Combine rice with tomato paste, which should coat the rice grains without drowning them. (In the finished dish, rice should be tinted orange; too much tomato paste will make it red.) Stir into the pot and continue to simmer, adding water sparingly to avoid burning. When meat, rice and vegetables are tender, Jollof Rice is ready to serve.

Variations: Eliminate meat for a good vegetarian main dish, and experiment with a variety of vegetables.

Chicken With Tomato Sauce · Rwanda

Serves 4

1 chicken, cut into pieces
3 tblsp. oil
1 onion, thinly sliced
3 large tomatoes, mashed
2 stalks of celery, cut into thin
   rounds
1 tsp. salt
1 hot pimento or chili pepper

Fry the chicken in hot oil until golden. Remove pieces and cook onions in the same pot. When they, too, are golden brown, return chicken pieces to the pot and add tomatos, celery, salt and hot pepper. Reduce heat and simmer until chicken is tender.

Kuku na Nazi · Kenya
Chicken with Coconut Milk

Serves 8-10. This dish from coastal east Africa uses both whole spices and curry powder.

2 3-lb. chickens, cut into pieces
5 inches fresh ginger, grated, or
   2 tblsp. ground ginger
20 small cloves garlic
2 hot chili peppers, or 1 tsp.
   cayenne pepper
1 medium onion, sliced
2 tblsp. oil
2 tblsp. curry powder
1/3 cup clarified butter (see
   recipe, page 9)
1 bunch of fresh coriander,
   chopped
1 tblsp. whole cumin seeds,
   pounded
4-6 cups coconut milk (see
   recipe, page 7)
1 cup coconut cream (see recipe,
   page 7)

Wash the chicken and pat it dry. Pound with a mortar and pestle, or purée in a blender or food processor, the ginger, garlic, chilies and curry powder. In a small skillet, sauté the onions in oil for 4-5 minutes, then add spice purée and simmer. Meanwhile, braise the chicken in butter in a large skillet or stew pot. When the chicken pieces are golden brown, transfer the onion/purée mixture to chicken pot. Add coriander, cumin and coconut milk, and cook until the chicken is tender. Pour coconut cream over the chicken, remove pot from the heat, and let stand until ready to serve. To eat, spoon over rice.

Badam/Kopra Murghi   South Africa
Coconut Chicken

Serves 4-6. Do try to use whole spices and fresh ginger in this exotic curry.

1 3-lb. chicken, cut into pieces
½ fresh coconut, grated (see
  page 6)
4 whole cloves, or ½ tsp. ground
  cloves
2 cardamom pods
3 cinnamon sticks, or 1 tsp.
  ground cinnamon
1 tsp. poppy seeds
½ tsp. cumin seeds, or ¼ tsp.
  ground cumin
1 tsp. ginger, grated, or ½ tsp.
  ground ginger
1 tsp. garlic, sliced
3 green chili peppers, or 1½ tsp.
  cayenne pepper
2 tblsp. cream
2 onions, diced
4 tblsp. clarified butter (see
  recipe, page 9) or oil
2 oz. peeled, slivered almonds
1 dozen pistachios, shelled

Wash and drain the chicken pieces. Purée all the other ingredients, except onions, butter and nuts in a blender or food processor. Or grind the spices manually and mix with cream. Fry the onions in butter or ghee just until golden. Remove from the pan, cool and crush with the back of a spoon. Then, brown chicken in the butter. Combine everything, including nuts, in a large baking dish. Cook in a 350° oven for 45 minutes, or until chicken is done.

Variation: Blend nuts along with other ingredients and proceed as directed.

Galinha à Zambeziana   Mozambique
Chicken Zambezia

Serves 4-6. From Mozambique's Zambezia province comes this spicy-hot chicken with coconut milk.

3-4 lbs. chicken pieces
piripiri sauce variation for chicken (see recipe, page 4)

Marinate (soak) the chicken pieces in piripiri sauce for at least two hours. (If you have time for them to marinate longer, cover and refrigerate.) To make the sauce, follow directions on page 4, leaving out the butter, and making sure that you use coconut milk instead of lemon juice, as specified in the variation for chicken.

When you're ready to cook, melt the cup of butter called for in the basting sauce and add it to the marinade. Use this mixture to coat chicken while it cooks. Either broil the chicken or grill it over a charcoal fire. To broil, lay pieces on a rack over a pan deep enough to catch the grease that will drip down. Cook 10-15 minutes on each side, basting several times with the sauce. When chicken is tender, serve with a fresh batch of piripiri sauce—made as before, but heated for five minutes before being passed around.

Special Occasion Dishes

These three recipes take more time and care than most, but once you prepare them, you'll want to repeat the experience.

Bstila   Morocco
Pigeon or Chicken Pie

Bstila is prepared traditionally with pigeon meat, but chicken is a good substitute.

Moroccans eat bstila with their fingers from a common bowl. If individual servings are preferred, cut into pie-shaped wedges. In a grand Moroccan feast, bstila would be only one of several courses, but for those to whom it is new, such elaborate fare ought to be the centerpiece of a meal.

This recipe is slightly adapted from Cooking in Morocco, *published in 1961 by The American Women's Association of Rabat. We have not tested it ourselves, but include it because it is a Moroccan classic. People who have tried it say it's worth the effort. Perhaps the closest North American equivalents to Moroccan pastry leaves are Greek phyllo pastry and strudel pastry.*

1 lb. blanched almonds
oil for browning
⅔ cup sugar
1 tblsp. cinnamon
2 tblsp. clarified butter (see
  recipe, page 9)
⅔ cup butter
1 large onion, minced
1 chicken, boned and cut in
  pieces
1 tsp. pepper
¼ tsp. salt
½ tsp. saffron
1 tsp. cinnamon
1 bunch parsley, chopped
½ bunch coriander, chopped
5 eggs
1½ lbs. "ouraka" (pastry leaves)
½ lb. butter, melted
powdered sugar

Brown the almonds in a little hot oil until golden. Pound coarsely with a mortar and pestle or put through a nut chopper. Add the sugar and cinnamon. Set aside.

Heat the two butters in a large, heavy pot over medium heat, then add the onion. Sauté for a few minutes and stir in the chicken, pepper, salt, saffron, cinnamon, parsley and coriander. Simmer gently until the chicken and sauce are well cooked. Add water to keep from burning if the juices boil down too fast. Remove the chicken.

Beat the eggs slightly and add gradually to the sauce, stirring constantly. Remove pot from the heat.

To assemble the bstila, butter a large round baking dish such as a pizza pan. Have all the ingredients at hand: pastry, melted butter, almond paste, chicken and sauce. Spread melted butter on one side of a pastry leaf and place, unbuttered side down, in the bottom of the pan. Do the same to 4 or 5 more leaves, arranging them around the pan in an overlapping cartwheel so that half of each leaf is lying outside of the pan. Using 4 or 5 more leaves, make a second, overlapping layer. Pour the sauce evenly over the pan-sized circle. Cover with two more layers of buttered leaves, 3 or 4 to a layer; this time don't let them hang outside the pan. Cover the pastry with the pieces of meat.

Next, lay down 2 more buttered pastry layers. Then, spread the almond mixture evenly across the surface. Take the pastry edges hanging outside and fold them up over the top. Finally, lay one leaf in the center of the top, buttered side down, and another 4 or 5, also buttered side down, in an overlapping cartwheel, as before. This time tuck the edges underneath, inside the pan edge, as though you were making a bed. Paint the top with butter. As the pastry cooks, all the buttered leaves will stick together.

Up to this point, bstila can be made ahead of time and refrigerated. Just before serving, brown for 30-40 minutes in a medium oven. After 15 or 20 minutes, when the top side is golden, remove from the oven and place a round oven-proof pan over it. Turn pie out carefully and put back in to brown the other side.

To serve, place on a large platter and sprinkle powdered sugar across the top. Then carefully make lines of cinnamon to form a grill pattern. Distribute small saucers of powdered sugar to be added individually at the table.

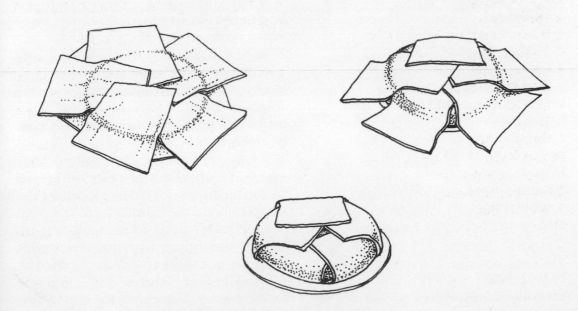

Yassa   Senegal

Serves 8-12. When you want to show a guest special honor, invite him or her for Yassa.

Here's how to serve and eat it the Senegalese way. When the chicken and rice is cool enough to handle, spread a cloth on the floor and put the full serving bowl in the center. Guests, having washed their hands, should remove shoes and sit or squat around the bowl. All guests take imaginary sections, like pieces of pie, directly in front of them as their own. It is generally impolite to reach into another person's area, although the center of the bowl is common to everyone.

The host usually will break up and distribute the meat, using the right hand, or individual eaters may break up the meat in their sections, pushing it toward the center. Because it would be extremely rude to put the left hand into the bowl, sometimes two people's hands are necessary for tearing the meat. (Tradition stipulates that the left hand is to be used for cleaning the body, and thus should not touch food.) To eat, gather a good amount of rice, chicken and sauce, and form into a ball against the side of the bowl. Squeeze it with your fingers until it is compact, then pop into your mouth. It is discourteous to start forming another ball while there is still food in your mouth.

When you have finished eating, clean off the part of the bowl in front of you with your hand, lick your hand clean, and go wash with soap and water. When you are through, it is polite to avoid looking at the face of someone who is still eating, although you may sit back down and converse.

1-2 chickens, cut up, including giblets
4-5 heads garlic
8-10 lbs. onions, sliced
1 cup red vinegar
2-3 fresh chili peppers
crushed dried chili peppers to taste
1 tblsp. black pepper
oil for frying
1-2 tblsp. soy sauce
5-8 cups brown or long-grain white rice
oil to coat pot

Wash the chicken pieces and pat them dry. Divide the garlic into cloves and crush. In a large stew pot, combine the onions, garlic, vinegar and spices. Add the chicken pieces. Stir well and let marinate (soak) in this mixture for at least an hour, or cover and refrigerate for several hours or overnight.

When you are ready to cook, remove chicken from the marinade and fry in oil until brown. Set the pieces aside. Next, remove the onions from the marinade and fry them in the same oil until they are light brown and somewhat limp. Return onions and chicken to the marinade and simmer until you are ready to eat (the longer the better). Add salt, pepper, and soy sauce to taste.

Meanwhile, coat the bottom of another large, heavy pot with a small amount of oil; heat it and lightly fry the rice. Add a little less than 2 cups of water for every cup of white rice and 3 cups water per cup if you use brown rice. Bring to a boil. Cover, turn down the heat and cook for 30 to 50 minutes, depending on the quantity of rice. Use a generous amount for the number of people eating. To serve, spread the rice a couple of inches deep in a wide, flat platter or bowl. Let cool for 5-10 minutes. Remove chicken pieces from the sauce and distribute evenly over the rice. Pour sauce over the dish as desired.

Biryani   # South Africa

Serves 8-10. Biryani is a dish of many parts. Although it takes a bit of time to put together, it is not at all difficult. Nor is it particularly rich, despite its full flavor. Even if you're serving fewer people, it's worth making this amount because the taste seems to improve with each reheating. For a larger gathering, the recipe may be doubled.

Basic ingredients:

2-3 lbs. chicken pieces
1 cup yogurt
2 tblsp. fresh tomato, minced
2 large onions, sliced
1 cup oil

2 cups lentils
2 cups rice
6 small potatoes, peeled
3 eggs, hard-boiled

Spices for marinating chicken:

1 tsp. ground ginger
1 tsp. garlic, sliced and crushed
¼ tsp. turmeric
2 pieces cinnamon
2 cardamom pods

3 green chili peppers
1 tsp. cumin
2 sprigs mint
1 tsp. ground coriander

Spices for cooking chicken:

1 piece cinnamon
2 cardamom pods
1 green chili pepper
1 tsp. cumin

1 tsp. ground coriander
1 tsp. fresh ginger, grated
1 clove garlic, slightly crushed

Spices for cooking rice:

2 cardamom pods
1 stick cinnamon

Rub chicken pieces with the ground ginger, garlic and turmeric. Place in a large bowl with the other marinating spices and the yogurt and tomato. In a heavy skillet, fry onion slices in a few tablespoons of the oil until just golden. Reserve two slices and set aside the skillet and oil. Crush the rest of the onion coarsely and add to the chicken/spice mixture. Stir to make sure all the chicken pieces are well-coated, and let sit for at least an hour.

Meanwhile, get out separate pots for cooking chicken, rice and lentils. Boil the lentils in 4 cups water, reduce heat, cover and simmer for 45 minutes (or use pre-cooked lentils). Boil the rice with cardamom and cinnamon in 4-5 cups of water, and here, again, reduce heat, cover and simmer. When rice is half-cooked, drain and set aside (timing will depend on the kind you're using; long-grain Basmati is preferred).

After the chicken has marinated, lift the pieces out and combine them with the chicken-cooking spices in a pot. Add 2-3 inches of water, cover, and simmer until meat can be removed easily from the bone. While it cooks, peel potatoes, chopping them into largish chunks. Fry in skillet used for the onions until the surfaces are crisp and golden brown. (The oil is hot enough if a test piece of potato sputters in the pan. Oil that is too cool will make the potatoes greasy.)

When everything is ready, put oil from the skillet and half the remaining fresh oil in the bottom of a large, heavy stew pot that has a tight-fitting lid. Scatter a handful of rice and all the lentils on the pot bottom. Distribute chicken and marinade across the lentils. Cover with potatoes and more rice. Over the rice place egg slices, then add the last of the rice. Top with the reserved rings of onion. Pour the rest of the oil and half a cup of cold water into the mixture. Cover the pot and cook over high heat for five minutes. Reduce heat, leaving contents to simmer for an hour. When serving, be sure to dig through all layers. Biryani should be accompanied by large amounts of yogurt and your choice of chutney.

Meat

Today, in much of Africa, meat of any kind is a luxury, but there is a long tradition of cookery that makes creative use of everything from camel to wildebeest. Although the recipes here call for the more familiar lamb, mutton, and beef, they are representative of the food many Africans enjoy during times when rainfall is adequate and livestock plentiful.

With the deletion of the meat, a number of these dishes can become delicious vegetarian fare.

Lamb Tagine with Artichokes   Morocco

Serves 6. This Moroccan lamb stew is quick to assemble and can simmer while you do other things.

2 lbs. stewing lamb
oil for frying
1 medium onion, sliced
2 medium tomatoes, chopped
¼ cup chopped parsley
¼ tsp. saffron or turmeric
1 tsp. salt
½ tsp. black pepper
½ tsp. ginger, grated, or ¼ tsp. ground ginger
¼ tsp. cinnamon
2 packages frozen artichoke hearts or hearts from 12 fresh artichokes

Chop the lamb into bite-size cubes, then sauté in oil in a large, heavy pot. (The oil is hot enough when a test piece of meat sputters.) Stir cubes to brown them on all sides. When well browned, add onion and continue to stir until onions are golden. Reduce heat to low and mix in the tomatoes, parsley, saffron or turmeric, salt, pepper, ginger and cinnamon. Simmer for 15 minutes, stirring occasionally before adding 1½ cups water along with the artichokes. Cook an additional 15-20 minutes if the hearts were frozen, and 35-40 minutes if they're fresh.

Lamb Tagine
with Onions and Raisins Morocco

Serves 6. The melding of the piquant flavors of onions, garlic or vinegar with the sweetness of fruit is as common to the stews of northern Africa as to the curries and chutneys of the south. As much as a cup of sugar is sometimes added to this tagine!

For the stew:

1 lamb shoulder, about 2 pounds	1 tsp. salt
oil for sautéing	1 tsp. parsley, finely chopped
2 large tomatoes, chopped	¼ tsp. saffron or turmeric
2 large onions, finely chopped	½ tsp. cinnamon
1 tsp. black pepper	

For the garnish:

1 lb. onions, sliced	2 tsp. cinnamon
2 tblsp. butter	1 tsp. pepper
1 cup raisins	

Put the meat in a large heavy pot whose bottom has been lightly coated with oil. Over high heat, brown the meat on all sides, especially the fatty areas. Lower heat to simmer; add onions, tomatoes, spices and half a cup of water. Cover and simmer for about 2 hours, stirring occasionally, until meat is fork tender.

To prepare the garnish: first sauté onions in butter until light brown. Add the raisins, cinnamon and pepper. Cook over low heat for 5 minutes, then add another half cup of water and bring to a boil. Reduce heat slightly and cook until liquid begins to thicken, stirring frequently. (If you choose, add a few teaspoons of sugar to caramelize the sauce.) Serve by ladling sauce over the stew. Eat with fresh bread or rice.

Tagine of String Beans, Tomatoes and Lamb

Morocco

Serves 6

2 lbs. stewing lamb, cut into
    bite-size pieces
2½ lbs. green beans, strung and
    halved
12 small tomatoes, peeled and
    coarsely chopped (see *About*
    peeling in the Introduction)
¼ cup oil
¼ tsp. saffron or ½ tsp. turmeric
2 tblsp. paprika
2 tsp. salt
3 cloves garlic, chopped
2 tblsp. lemon juice

Pre-heat oven to 300°. Combine all ingredients except lemon juice in a heavy baking dish. Cover with foil or a tight-fitting lid and bake for an hour. Add lemon juice, reduce heat to 200°, and continue to cook uncovered another hour, or until meat is very tender.

Bamia

Egypt

Lamb and Okra Stew

Serves 4

1 lb. lamb, cubed
2-4 tblsp. olive oil
2 lbs. fresh or frozen okra
    (thawed)
1 large onion, finely chopped
3 cloves garlic, thinly sliced
1 tsp. salt
½ tsp. pepper
3 large tomatoes
1 tsp. coriander seeds, crushed
juice of 1 lemon

Pre-heat oven to 350°. In a heavy skillet, brown the lamb in hot oil. Add the okra, stirring quickly for 2-3 minutes. Remove meat pieces and okra and put in onions, garlic, salt and pepper. After 2-3 more minutes, reduce heat and add the tomato, coriander and lemon juice plus 1½ cups water. (Instead of water, you may use broth or vegetable stock.) Simmer 8-10 minutes. Combine meat/okra mixture and contents of skillet in an oven-proof dish. Bake for an hour, or until meat is cooked and okra is tender.

Stuffed Vine Leaves   Egypt

Vine leaves can be purchased in ethnic or gourmet shops. If they have been canned or bottled in brine, you will need to pour it off and draw out the excess salt. To do so, cover leaves with boiling water, and let them sit for 20 minutes. Drain, then soak in cold water and drain again. Leaves can be stuffed a day ahead, refrigerated, and cooked just before serving. Preparation time is about 1 hour to stuff and an hour and a half to cook.

½ lb. vine leaves
⅔ cup long grain rice
1 lb. ground lamb or beef
1 medium onion, finely chopped
3 tblsp. parsley, chopped
¼ tsp. black pepper
2 tsp. tomato paste
3 tblsp. melted butter, divided
2 cloves garlic, cut into slivers
juice of 1 lemon

Soak leaves, if necessary; then line a baking pan with a layer of leaves.

Meanwhile, cook the rice in boiling water for 5 minutes, drain, and mix with the meat, onion, parsley, pepper, tomato paste, and half of the butter. To stuff a leaf, lay it on the counter, vein side up, with its stem pointing towards you. Remove stem with a small, sharp knife. You can gauge the amount of filling required by the size of the leaf—about a tablespoon for a large leaf, and half that amount for smaller ones. Shape the filling into an oval on the lower (stem) portion. Fold the bottom of the leaf up over the filling, and the sides in towards the middle, overlapping them. Then roll up from the bottom into a tight cylinder.

As you stuff the leaves, lay them in the pan, packing them closely so they don't unravel. Continue preparing leaves in this manner until all the stuffing is used. Insert slivers of garlic between the rolls, and sprinkle with the rest of the melted butter and the lemon juice. Pour in about 1 cup water— enough almost to cover the leaves. Seal the pan with a lid or foil. Cook on medium heat for about an hour and a half, until the meat is cooked and well-browned. Check periodically. If the water evaporates, it may be necessary to add more during the cooking. Serve leaves on a large platter, accompanied by yogurt sauce or plain yogurt.

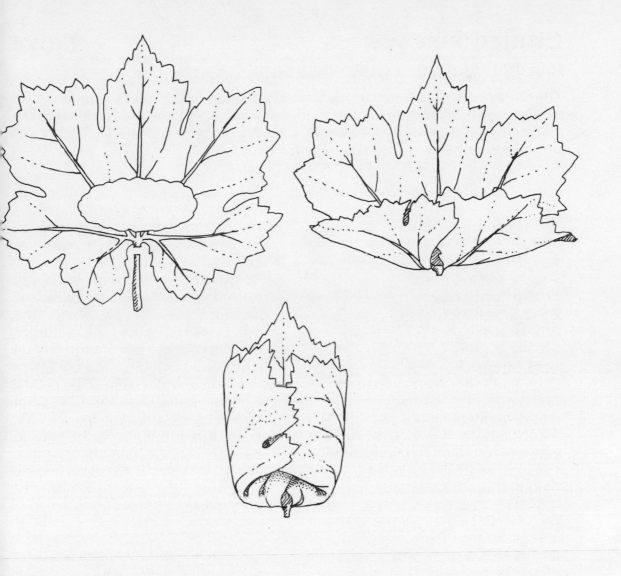

Yogurt Sauce for Vine Leaves   Egypt

This sauce is as good on Moroccan beef brochettes or Tanzanian combo flat-cakes as it is over vine leaves.

2 cups plain yogurt
1-2 cloves garlic, minced and
   crushed

salt and pepper to taste
3 tblsp. fresh mint, chopped or 1
   tblsp. dried mint

   Mix all the ingredients together in a serving bowl.

Lamb Couscous   Libya
Lamb, Onion and Chickpea Stew

Although it has three separate elements, this couscous recipe is a good choice for entertaining, because two of the three can be made ahead of time; only the couscous needs last-minute attention. And you can vary the ingredients to serve as few or as many guests as you like.

For the meat and vegetable base:

¼-½ lb. stewing lamb per person
1 large or 2 medium onions
olive oil for frying
3 tblsp. tomato paste
2 tblsp. turmeric
3-5 chili peppers
1 tblsp. salt
1 tblsp. cumin
2 tsp. fenugreek seeds
2 tsp. coriander seeds, crushed
1 tsp. ground allspice (or a mixture of cinnamon, cloves and nutmeg)
At least 4 of your choice of the following vegetables: carrots, pumpkin, winter or summer squash, potatoes, turnips, leeks

For the chickpea sauce:

1 oz. dried chickpeas per person, pre-soaked
1 large onion for every 2 people
pinch of salt
olive oil for frying

The lamb stew can be made with different cuts of lamb—neck, breast, shoulder—as the bones and cartilage give more flavor and richness to the broth.

Brown the meat and onions in enough hot olive oil to cover the bottom of a large stew pot. Add tomato paste, spices and water to cover. Let the mixture simmer for an hour before adding your choice of vegetables, which should be peeled and cut into large chunks. Root vegetables will take longest to cook, so add them first. Summer squash will only need about 15 minutes. Add more water if necessary, taste for seasonings, and cook until the vegetables are tender.

Simmer the chickpeas in plain water until tender—2 hours or longer, depending on the peas. An alternate method is to cook them in your oven at its lowest setting for several hours. (If you are pressed for time, you can substitute canned chickpeas.) Slice the onions thinly, then salt and sauté them gently in olive oil until limp. Add a little of the broth from the lamb stew and simmer, covered, for 20 minutes. Add drained chickpeas and cook for 20 more minutes.

For the couscous:

For tips on cooking couscous, see *Grains and Bread* chapter.

2 oz. dry couscous per person
 salt

To assemble and serve: In a large bowl or deep platter, spread and fluff up the hot grain. Pour on broth from the stew until the couscous is lightly coated. Distribute the onion and chickpea mixture evenly over the surface. Then arrange the meat and vegetables in the center and sprinkle lightly with ground cloves or allspice. Serve more broth separately.

Couscous   Tunisia

Serves 6-8. This version of couscous is no less delicious for being quick and easy.

4 lbs. lamb, chopped into pieces
   (neck pieces with bones are
   good)
3-4 large onions, chopped
½ cup olive oil
6 oz. tomato paste
2 cups fresh tomatoes
1 tblsp. ground cumin
1 tsp. black pepper
1 tsp. curry powder
1 tsp. cayenne pepper
5 cloves garlic
salt to taste
2 green bell peppers, coarsely
   chopped
1 large butternut squash
4 medium turnips, chopped into
   medium-size pieces
4 carrots, chopped into medium-
   size strips
1 lb. onions, chopped finely
1 lb. potatoes

2 cups dry couscous, cooked (see
   couscous section in *Grains
   and Bread* chapter)
2 green onions, chopped
3 sprigs of parsley, chopped
1-2 lemons

In a large stew pot, brown the lamb and the first group of onions in olive oil. Add tomato paste and cook for 5 minutes, stirring frequently. Mix in the tomatoes, spices, and green peppers, and reduce the heat to simmer. After 15 minutes, add the remaining ingredients, except couscous, plus enough water to bring the liquid level to within 3 inches of the tops of the vegetables. Cook until meat and vegetables are tender. Serve on individual plates by ladling over couscous. Garnish each serving with chopped green onions, parsley and a wedge of lemon.

Lamb Couscous — Algeria
Lamb, Meatball and Chickpea Stew

Five different components form this lavish dish. It differs from the Libyan recipe in that it reflects a French influence.

For the meat and vegetable base (per person):

1 piece chicken
1 lamb or mutton rib chop
olive oil for frying
½ onion, sliced
½ leek, sliced
pinch of paprika
1 clove garlic, crushed
chicken stock (optional)
1 tblsp. tomato paste
sprig of parsley
2 bay leaves
pinch of thyme
salt and pepper to taste
basil and cumin (see directions below)
½ carrot, sliced
½ turnip or potato, sliced
½ summer squash, sliced
fresh mint (optional)

Brown the meats in a large stew pot, using a small amount of oil, then remove the pieces and set aside. In the same pot, soften the onions and leeks. Add the paprika and garlic and stir in. Return the meat and cover with water or chicken stock. Add the tomato paste, parsley, bay leaves, a good pinch of thyme, and salt and pepper to taste. The amount of basil and cumin depends on the total volume of your stew. Start out with substantial pinches of each and taste the mixture after it has cooked for 15 or 20 minutes. Judge by whether you find it flavorful enough. Add the vegetables about 45 minutes before the stew is ready, except for the squash which should be added 20 minutes before serving. Total cooking time will be about an hour and a half, although a stewing hen and mutton might need as long as 3 hours.

When fresh mint is available, add a sprig 10 minutes before cooking is finished.

For the meatballs
(for every 4 people):

8 oz. ground beef or lamb
1 small onion, finely chopped
1 thin slice of bread, soaked in
    milk and squeezed dry
1 tblsp. parsley, finely chopped
1 tblsp. peanut oil
pinch of saffron
pinch of ginger
pinch of nutmeg
flour
1 egg, beaten
oil for frying

Mix together all the ingredients except flour, egg, and oil for frying. Form mixture into smallish rounds about the size of ping-pong balls. Roll each ball in flour and then in the beaten egg. Fry in a small amount of hot oil until brown. Drain away the oil and add just enough water from the stew pot to cover the balls. Simmer for 20 minutes.

For the chickpeas:

1 oz. dry chickpeas per person

For cooking instructions, see *About grains* in the Introduction.

For the harissa (hot sauce):

Hot chilies, crushed
 peanut oil

Crush as many hot peppers as you like into pieces and cover them with peanut oil. Stored in a cool, dry place, the mixture keeps a very long time and becomes hotter as it ages.

For the couscous:

2 oz. dry couscous per person

For cooking instructions, see couscous section in *Grains and Bread* chapter.

To serve, select a flat bowl or a large platter that has sloping edges. Put in the prepared couscous and moisten with a bit of stock from the stew pot. Arrange chickpeas evenly over the surface. Distribute the meats and vegetables across the top, moistening with a bit more stock. The remaining stock and the harissa should be passed separately at the table.

Lamb Couscous   Mauritania

Serves 6-8. You might encounter this type of sweet/savory dish all over north-west Africa, where it is as likely to be made with goat or camel meat as with lamb. The vegetables will be whatever is available. Try it over plain couscous or with the fancier version below.

For the stew:

2 lbs. lamb, cut into small chunks
a few tblsp. of olive oil
2 onions, chopped
3 cloves garlic, thinly sliced
3-4 turnips, peeled and chopped
4 carrots, sliced

3 small potatoes, quartered
1 cup cabbage, coarsely chopped
1-2 winter squash, peeled and
   chopped, or 1 cup pumpkin,
   chopped
2 medium tomatoes

For the couscous:

2 lbs. dry couscous grain
1 cup dates, pitted and chopped
½ cup raisins

8 oz. chickpeas, pre-cooked
¼ cup butter or olive oil

In a large stew pot that has a tight-fitting lid, brown the meat by stirring quickly in hot oil or butter. Reduce heat and sauté the onions and garlic until golden. Add vegetables, stirring for 2-3 minutes. Cover with about 2 cups water, put the lid on the pot, and simmer until vegetables are tender and meat is cooked. Mix the dates, raisins, and chickpeas into the dry couscous, and steam. (See couscous section in *Grains and Bread* chapter.) Serve by ladling the stew over couscous on individual plates.

Jollof Rice   Mali

Serves 4. Jollof Rice is a popular dish in much of west Africa. One of its many variations is this version from Mali.

3 large tomatoes
2 tblsp. tomato paste
2 large onions, one chopped,
    one sliced
1 chili pepper, or ½ tsp. cayenne
    pepper
¼ cup peanut oil
2 cloves garlic, sliced
1 lb. lamb, cut into 1-inch cubes
salt and pepper to taste
your choice of vegetables
    (optional)
1 cup dry rice, cooked

Peel tomatoes by plunging them into boiling water for 2 minutes, and then immediately into cold water. Slip the skin off, and mash well with a fork. Combine with tomato paste and set aside. Brush the onion slices with a tablespoon or so of the oil, then broil in the oven for 3 minutes or until brown (being careful not to burn them). Grind, pound, or use a blender or food processor to blend the broiled onions and the chili or cayenne to a paste. Set aside.

In a heavy skillet over medium heat, fry chopped onion in the oil until golden. Add garlic, followed by meat, stirring frequently until cubes are browned on all sides. Reduce heat to simmer and stir in the tomato sauce. Add the onion/chili paste, along with salt and pepper and about a cup of water. If using vegetables, put them in now. Stir well and simmer over low heat about 45 minutes, or until meat is cooked. Mix with rice to serve.

Loubya Khadra Marqa   Algeria
Green Beans in Lamb Sauce

Serves 4-6

½ lb. stewing lamb
4 tblsp. olive oil
3 medium-size onions, thinly
   sliced
1 stick cinnamon
1 tsp. turmeric
1 tsp. salt
pinch of black pepper
2 tsp. cayenne pepper
3 large tomatoes
2 lbs. green beans, broken into 2
   pieces each
3 sprigs parsley

Using a fairly large pot, brown the meat in moderately hot oil. Add, one at a time—stirring for a minute or so between each addition—3 or 4 slices of onion, and the cinnamon, turmeric, salt and peppers.

If you want to cook this dish as an Algerian would, you must peel the tomatoes (see *About peeling* in the Introduction). In any case, chop them, and add a few pieces to the pot, along with about a cup of water. Reduce heat and simmer for 3 or 4 minutes. Stir in the green beans and the remaining tomatoes and onions. Finally, add the parsley.

Simmer, covered, over low heat until the meat pulls apart easily, about 30 minutes. Before serving, uncover and raise the temperature to allow some of the liquid to evaporate and the sauce to thicken slightly. But watch the pot carefully, and stir as necessary to prevent burning and sticking.

Skudahkharis
Lamb and Rice

Somalia

Serves 4

1 lb. lamb, cut into bite-size chunks
½ cup cooking oil
1 onion, thinly sliced
2 tomatoes, chopped
1 large clove garlic, minced
2 sprigs parsley
1 tsp. cumin
3 whole cloves
1 stick cinnamon
3 cardamom pods
1 tsp. salt
3 oz. tomato paste
2 cups rice, uncooked

In a large, heavy pot, brown the meat in heated oil. Add onion slices, and stir for several minutes, then add tomatoes. While the mixture simmers over low heat, crush garlic, parsley and all the spices together, using a mortar and pestle, blender or food processor; or grind everything between 2 stones. Add to the pot.

Thin tomato paste with about ⅓ cup warm water. Stir into the pot, along with the 2 cups rice. Immediately add 4 cups boiling water and stir well. Cover, then simmer until rice is done and has absorbed most or all of the water, about 20-30 minutes. (Brown rice will take 15 minutes longer and will need an additional cup of water.)

Beef Brochettes   Morocco

Serves 4-6

2 lbs. beef or lamb, cubed in
  bite-size pieces
1 medium-size onion, finely
  chopped
10 sprigs parsley, chopped
1 tsp. salt
¾ tsp. black pepper
2 tsp. paprika
1 tsp. cumin
1 tblsp. vinegar
1 tblsp. olive oil

Combine all the ingredients in a large mixing bowl. Stir to mix well and refrigerate at least 8 hours or overnight. When you are ready to cook, spear 5 or 6 pieces of meat on skewers. Broil over a charcoal fire until done to your liking. In Morocco, these brochettes are served with French bread and a spicy-hot tomato sauce. Make your own by blending 4 tablespoons of tomato paste with 2 of olive oil, and adding 4 tablespoons of vinegar, 2 of water, 1 teaspoon salt and Tabasco sauce to taste.

Combo Flatcake   Tanzania

½ lb. lean ground beef
3 large potatoes, peeled and
  grated
3 large carrots, grated
½ cup whole wheat flour
2 tblsp. sugar
½ tsp. salt
1 tsp. curry powder
½ tsp. cinnamon
1 tsp. baking powder
1 egg
½ cup milk
¼ cup vegetable oil

Combine beef, potatoes and carrots in a large bowl. In another bowl, sift together the flour, sugar, salt, curry powder, cinnamon and baking powder. Add to the beef mixture, along with the egg and milk. Blend thoroughly. Into a heavy skillet over medium heat, put 2 tablespoons of salad oil. Dump the mixture into the pan in half-cup portions, as many as will fit at one time, flattening each slightly with a wooden spoon. Cook, covered, for 5 minutes or until browned. Flip cakes over to brown the second side. Repeat until all the mixture is used, adding the remaining oil, a bit at a time, to prevent sticking. Makes 8-10 cakes.

Geema Kerrie
South Africa
Ground Meat Curry

Serves 4-6. "True" curries use a blend of spices tailored to each dish rather than a purchased curry powder. This adaptation has the advantage of being simple and fast.

2 lbs. ground beef or lamb
3 small onions, chopped
¼ cup oil
2 tblsp. fresh ginger, grated
4 cloves garlic
½ tsp. salt
2 large tomatoes
2 chili peppers
2 tblsp. curry powder
½ tblsp. turmeric
1 tblsp. ghurum masala (see
  recipe, page 6)

Brown meat over moderate heat. Set aside. In a separate large skillet, gently fry onions in oil just until golden brown. Meanwhile, pound or grind the ginger and garlic into a paste. When onions are ready, add to skillet the ginger/garlic paste, salt, tomatoes, chilies, curry powder and turmeric. Finally, stir in the meat and continue simmering for about 20 minutes, or until well cooked. Remove from heat, mix in ghurum masala, and serve with rice or Indian bread (see *Grains and Bread* chapter).

Malay Influences

Of the many groups who have influenced South Africa's cuisine, none has had greater impact than the Malays who were brought as slaves for 17th-century Dutch settlers. The boboties, sosaties and bredies that are among the foods thought of as *typically* South African are all of Malay origin.

Biryani   South Africa
Meat with Rice and Lentils

Serves 4-6. This is a simpler version of the special-occasion biryani in the Chicken chapter.

1 lb. beef, cut in two-inch cubes
½ cup yogurt
1 tsp. cayenne pepper
½ tsp. turmeric
1 tsp. salt
¾ tsp. cumin
¾ tsp. coriander
2 cloves garlic, minced
1 tsp. fresh ginger, grated
1 large onion, thinly sliced
½ cup oil or clarified butter (see
  recipe, page 9)
1½ cups long-grain rice
½ cup lentils
2 hard-boiled eggs, sliced
sprigs of parsley or coriander
  leaves, chopped

Combine meat with yogurt and all the spices and leave to marinate for 2-3 hours. When you're ready to cook, fry the onion in a large stew pot with half the butter. Add the marinated meat mixture and simmer until liquid is slightly thickened. Set aside.

Meanwhile, in separate pots, using enough water to cover, boil rice and lentils for about 15 minutes. Drain. To assemble the biryani, layer the ingredients in the pot: rice first, then meat, more rice, lentils, and meat again. Continue in this pattern until everything has been used. Melt the remaining butter and pour over the mixture along with ½ cup water. Cover the pot and simmer on lowest heat for one hour. Serve on a platter, garnished with parsley or coriander and egg slices.

Bobotie   South Africa

Serves 6

2 onions, finely chopped
2 lbs. ground beef
1 slice bread
1 cup milk
1 tblsp. curry powder
1½ tblsp. sugar
½ cup raisins
3 tblsp. chutney
2 tsp. salt
½ tsp. pepper
½ tblsp. turmeric
2 tblsp. vinegar or lemon juice
6 almonds, quartered
1 egg
4 bay leaves, or peel of 1 lemon,
    grated

Pre-heat oven to 350°. Sauté beef with onions until meat is brown. (If beef is very lean, you may need to grease the skillet.) Soak the bread in half the milk; then mash the slice with a fork.

Combine all the ingredients except the egg, remaining milk, and the bay leaves. (If you're using lemon peel, go ahead and mix it in.) Spread the mixture in a greased casserole and tuck in the bay leaves here and there. Bake for 1 hour, then beat the egg with the remaining half-cup of milk and pour over the casserole. Return to oven for another half hour. Serve with rice and chutney.

Kerrieboontjies   Southern Africa
Curried Beans

Serves 4-6

3 onions, thinly sliced
2-3 tblsp. oil
2 lbs. ribs or shoulder of lamb,
    cut into pieces
salt and pepper to taste
1 green chili pepper, crushed
2 cloves garlic, crushed
1 tsp. curry powder
2 lbs. kidney, pinto, or navy
    beans, pre-cooked
lemon juice

In a heavy stew pot, brown onion in oil until golden yellow. Add meat, salt and pepper. Sauté over medium heat until meat loses its red color, then cook over low heat for 15-20 more minutes. With two stones or a mortar and pestle, grind or pound the chili and garlic together; add them, with the curry powder, to the pot. Continue simmering until meat is tender, adding the beans about 15 minutes before serving. When the flavors have blended, transfer to a serving dish and drizzle with lemon juice.

Tomato Bredie
Tomato Stew

South Africa

Serves 4-6. When bredies are mentioned to a South African, it is likely to be this variety that comes to mind first. Try to use vine-ripened tomatoes.

2 lbs. stewing lamb
2 large onions, sliced
2 tblsp. oil
8 large tomatoes, peeled (see
  About peeling in the Introduction), and sliced into rounds
  about ¼-inch thick
1 tsp. sugar
1 tsp. salt
1 chili pepper, finely chopped, or
  ½ tsp. cayenne pepper
1 clove garlic, crushed

In a heavy pot or large skillet, brown the meat and onions in moderately hot oil until lamb is seared on all sides and onions are golden. Then simmer, over lowest heat, for about 30 minutes.

If fat from meat has accumulated in the pot, pour off all but about 2 tablespoons. Add tomatoes and remaining ingredients. Simmer, covered, for one hour, stirring frequently enough to prevent mixture from sticking. Uncover, skim off any excess fat, and cook several more minutes until sauce is very thick.

Serve with rice.

Green Bean Bredie   South Africa
Green Bean Stew

Serves 4-6

2 large onions, thinly sliced
2 lbs. rib of mutton, diced
2 tblsp. oil
1 lb. green beans, sliced
   lengthwise
½ tblsp. sugar
½ tblsp. salt
1 chili pepper, crushed
6 medium potatoes, peeled and
   halved

Fry onions and mutton in oil over medium heat, stirring constantly to prevent burning. When lamb is evenly browned, add the beans, sugar, salt, and chili; pour in 1 cup water and simmer gently for an hour. Put in the potatoes and cook another hour, or until meat is tender.

Serve with rice.

Pumpkin Bredie   South Africa
Pumpkin Stew

Serves 6-8

3-4 lbs. stewing lamb or mutton,
   cut into pieces
2 tblsp. oil
4 onions, sliced
2 red peppers, chopped
6 cups raw pumpkin, diced
salt and pepper to taste
pinch of cinnamon
pinch of nutmeg
1 tsp. sugar
1 bay leaf
piece of orange peel

In a large skillet or stew pot, brown the meat in the oil. Remove pieces and set aside. Using the same pot, lightly sauté onions and peppers until tender. Return the meat to the cook pot, along with the remaining ingredients. Cover with 1 cup water and simmer until tender—about an hour for lamb, and 2 or 3 times that for mutton.

Serve with rice.

Sosaties   Southern Africa

Serves 6. "Come to a braai" means barbeque time in South Africa. Sosaties are classic fare at a braaivleis, *or outdoor grill. Traditionally, a braai was considered complete with just sosaties, freshly-baked bread, and the large, round sausages called* boerewors *(literally, Boer sausage). You must begin preparing the sosaties 12-14 hours ahead of time.*

3 lbs. boneless lamb
1 clove garlic, split
salt and pepper to taste
4 medium onions, finely
   chopped
2 tblsp. oil
1½ tsp. ground coriander
½ tsp. ground cumin
1 heaping tsp. hot curry powder
   (see recipe, page 5)
1 tblsp. brown sugar
½ cup fresh lemon juice
2 tblsp. apricot jam
2 bay leaves or fresh lemon
   leaves
2 tblsp. flour

Rub the lamb with garlic, then cut it into bite-size cubes. Place the pieces in a dish and sprinkle them with salt and pepper. Meanwhile, fry the onions in oil until golden. Stir in the coriander, cumin, and curry powder, followed 2-3 minutes later by the brown sugar, lemon juice and jam. Add ½ cup water. Bring to a quick boil, stirring constantly. Remove from heat. When the mixture is thoroughly cooled, pour it over the meat, stick in the bay or lemon leaves, then cover the bowl and refrigerate overnight or at least 12 hours.

At the cookout, thread meat on skewers and grill over hot coals. Save the marinade in which the meat was soaked. (For an indoor meal, lay skewers on a grill or slotted tray over a pan to catch drippings. Broil in the oven.) The lamb will cook in 10-15 minutes.

While the meat grills, transfer the marinade to a heavy pot, first removing the leaves. Bring to a boil. For a thicker sauce, spoon out a bit of the hot liquid to blend with flour. Whisk into a smooth paste and stir gradually into the pan. Pass sauce separately to pour over the meat.

Seafood

With some 20,000 miles of coastline, Africa has a long tradition of small boats venturing far from shore in search of culinary treasures. The Mediterranean, the Atlantic, the Indian Ocean and the Red Sea border 33 countries, while salt water completely surrounds another seven island nations. In the continental interior, mighty rivers like the Nile and the Congo and great waters like Lake Victoria yield their bounty to the skilled and the diligent.

Fresh seafood is tossed into soups and stews, eaten with a variety of grains, made into flavorful sauces, or simply grilled with butter. Salt-drying and pickling preserve the catch for another day. These recipes are a sampling of Africa's most common fish and seafood dishes.

Seafood Soups

Not quite thick enough to be called stews, these blends of seafood and vegetables are main dishes, nevertheless. They are meant to be served with large amounts of rice or stiff porridge (see recipes in the *Grains and Bread* chapter). If you prefer less carbohydrates and more fish per person, you may want to double the recipes to serve the stated number of people.

Caldo de Peixe   Cape Verde
Fish Soup

Serves 6-8. In Cape Verde, this soup is thickened by the addition of both "mandioca"—a flour made from manioc, and "farinha de pau"—crushed, dried bread crumbs. Manioc flour is not as unfamiliar as it might sound. It's the same thing as tapioca flour, made from the starchy tuber known variously as manioc or cassava. If you can't find tapioca flour, you can substitute quick-cooking, or "minute" tapioca.

1 tsp. salt
2-3 green (unripe) bananas, sliced in rounds
1 yellow onion, sliced
4 tblsp. olive oil
2 cloves garlic
1 bay leaf
1 chili pepper or ½ tsp. cayenne pepper
1 bunch parsley, finely chopped
2 large tomatoes, chopped
¼ cup tapioca flour
¼ cup dry bread crumbs
½ of a small cabbage, chopped
4-6 large potatoes, chopped in chunks
4-6 sweet potatoes, chopped in chunks
2 lbs. fish, without bones

In a mixing bowl, dissolve salt in enough water to cover the banana pieces. Dump them in, and soak for 10-15 minutes to draw out the "pucker" quality of the unripe fruit.

Meanwhile, in a deep skillet or heavy stew pot, brown onion in oil over moderate heat. Add garlic, bay leaf, pepper, parsley and tomato, and sauté for several minutes, stirring frequently. Stir in 4 cups hot water.

In a separate bowl, use a bit of the hot broth to whisk the tapioca flour into a thin, smooth paste. Bring soup almost to a boil and add the paste and bread crumbs, stirring vigorously. Immediately reduce heat to simmer.

Drain the bananas and add them, along with the cabbage and potatoes. Gently lay in the fish, cover with water, and simmer for 20-30 minutes, or until everything is done.

Caldo de Camarâo

Cape Verde

Fresh Shrimp Soup

Serves 6-8

2 green (unripe) bananas, sliced
   in rounds
1 tsp. salt
3 lbs. fresh shrimp (unshelled,
   with heads, if possible)
pinch of salt
1 large onion, sliced
2 tblsp. olive oil
2 large garlic cloves, crushed
3 medium tomatoes, chopped
3 chili peppers, chopped or
   crushed, or 1 tsp. cayenne
   pepper
4 medium potatoes, chopped in
   chunks

Dissolve the salt in enough water to cover the banana pieces. Soak them in the salt water for 10-15 minutes to draw out the "pucker" quality of the unripe fruit.

Meanwhile, wash the shrimp in cold, running water, but don't shell or remove heads. Cook in 2 cups of boiling, salted water for 6-8 minutes. Then peel off shells and remove heads. Save heads and cooking water.

In a large, heavy skillet or stew pot, sauté the onion in oil over moderate heat until golden. Stir in garlic, tomatoes and pepper. Add shrimp.

If you have shrimp heads, push them through a sieve. Stir into the pot along with the water in which they cooked. Drain bananas and add them, with the potatoes, and cook until everything is tender, about 20 minutes, adding enough water for the number of servings you want. Serve with a stiff porridge (see recipes in *Grains and Bread* chapter).

Abenkwan
Palm Nut Soup

Ghana

This soup would seem merely greasy without the characteristic orange tint and unique flavor provided by palm oil. Unless you can find some in an ethnic or specialty grocery, you shouldn't try this recipe; no substitute oils are appropriate. Serves 4.

2 cups palm oil
1 cup onions, chopped
1 chili pepper, crushed, or ½ tsp. cayenne pepper
2 cups tomato, chopped
2 cups okra
1 medium eggplant, cut into chunks
1 lb. fish or crab meat
½ tsp. salt

In a large, heavy stew pot, boil the palm oil for 10 minutes. Add onions and pepper and continue cooking on high heat for another 5 minutes. Reduce heat, add remaining ingredients, and simmer for an hour or more until soup is somewhat thickened. Stir from time to time. If there is too much palm oil on the surface for your liking, skim it off with a large spoon before serving.

Fish

Fresh, salt-dried or pickled, fish is an excellent source of protein, and often is good value as well. Although baking is not a common cooking method in most of Africa, several of these recipes have been adapted for your ovens. When you want greater authenticity, try grilling or sautéeing instead.

For recipes specifying dried, salted fish, look for such widely-available varieties as cod, herring and mackerel. All should be soaked in fresh water for several hours or overnight to leach out the excess salt. Changing the water periodically will aid the process.

In western fish markets, smoked fish comes in two basic varieties: cold-smoked and hot-smoked. The former, cured slowly over a smoldering fire, is primarily a preservation method, while the latter is a way of adding flavor during cooking. You may use either kind in recipes calling for smoked fish, as long as you remember that the cold-smoked kind needs cooking, and the hot-smoked variety is ready-to-eat and highly perishable. Among the most common cold-smoked fish are haddock, called *finnan haddie*, and herring, called *kippered herring*. Smoked salmon or whitefish generally has been hot-smoked and needs no further cooking

Molho Cru   Angola
Sauce for Fish and Seafood

Makes about ½ cup

2 cloves garlic, crushed
½ cup green onions, including
    tops, snipped
4 tblsp. parsley, finely chopped
1 tsp. ground cumin
¼ tsp. salt
4 tblsp. vinegar
4 tblsp. water

Combine, then grind or process all ingredients into a paste. Chill. Serve over fish or other seafood.

Fish with Pepper Sauce   Ghana

This recipe begins with cooked fish. Bake, broil or sauté any variety you like, and, if necessary, remove the bones. Served the west African way with lots of stiff porridge, these amounts will feed 4.

4 medium tomatoes, quartered
2 medium onions, quartered
1 tsp. salt
2 tblsp. chili peppers, coarsely
　chopped
1 lb. fish, cooked

Purée the tomatoes, onions, salt, and peppers in a blender or food processor just long enough to make the mixture uniformly smooth. Blend gently with fish in a cooking pot, and heat through at a low temperature, being careful not to let the mixture boil. Serve with rice or a stiff porridge (see recipes in *Grains and Bread* chapter).

Variation: Substitute a pound of sardines for the fish.

Mtuzi wa Samaki   Kenya
Baked Curried Fish

Serves 4

2 lbs. white fish, bones removed
3 large yellow onions, sliced
2 tblsp. oil
2 chili peppers or 1 tsp. cayenne
　pepper
3 cloves garlic
4 medium-size tomatoes, or 6 oz.
　tomato paste
½ cup white vinegar
½ tsp. ground cardamom
½ tsp. cumin
½ tsp. salt

Preheat oven to 350°. Lay the fish in a baking pan. Heat oil to a moderate temperature, and fry the onion slices until transparent. Arrange over the fish.

Combine the remaining ingredients in a blender or food processor until smooth. (Or crush chilies and garlic with a mortar and pestle and mash tomatoes well with a fork before combining with other ingredients.) Pour over fish, cover the pot, and simmer about 30 minutes until fish is just cooked.

Pastel com Diabo Dentro Cape Verde
Pastry with the Devil Inside

Makes 14-16. "Unusual" might be the word you'd choose to describe these tuna-filled turnovers after your first taste. But we predict that a few more bites will change your reaction to "fantastic."

Be sure to use fresh tuna if you can get it. For corn flour, check natural foods groceries, or make your own by grinding corn meal in a food processor until it is extremely fine. (Some grocery stores carry a finely-ground meal that needs no further processing.) Plan to serve 3-4 turnovers per person.

2 large sweet potatoes, unpeeled
1-2 cups corn flour
1 medium onion, finely chopped
2 tblsp. olive oil
1 lb. fresh tuna, cooked, or 1
   7-oz. can of tuna
1 medium tomato, chopped
2 chili peppers, finely chopped,
   or 1 tsp. cayenne pepper
1 tsp. salt
oil for deep frying

To make the pastry, wash potatoes well and boil them until they are very tender. Spin them, skins and all, in a blender or food processor until they make a smooth paste, or mash them thoroughly in a large bowl, making sure to get out all the lumps. Slowly add the corn flour, blending it in with your hands or with a wooden spoon to make a stiff dough. The moisture in your potatoes will determine how much you need, but the mixture should resemble biscuit dough or pie pastry (although it will be somewhat coarser). If the dough becomes too dry, add a few spoons of the water in which the potatoes were cooked. Roll into a ball, wrap in a damp, lint-free cloth, and chill while you make the filling.

Sauté onions in oil until they become transparent. Flake the tuna and mix with the onions and the remaining ingredients. (If you like spicy food, you may want to double or triple the amount of hot pepper.) Unwrap the dough and spread the damp towel on a flat surface. Working on top of it, tear off golf-ball size pieces of the dough and roll them into circles about ⅛-inch thick and 4-5 inches in diameter. Put a tablespoonful of the tuna filling on half of the dough circle; fold the other half of the circle across it and pinch the edges to seal.

In a deep, heavy pot, heat oil for frying until a test piece of dough sputters vigorously. You may either deep-fry the turnovers (see *About frying* in the Introduction) or fry them in a couple of inches of oil, turning them once to allow both sides to cook. Fry 2 or 3 at a time, continuing to make more as you fry the first ones. The oil is the right temperature when a test turnover becomes golden brown after frying about 3 minutes on each side. Drain on clean, absorbent cloths, and serve immediately.

Riz au Poisson

Senegal

Rice with Fish

Serves 4-6

For the fish paste:

2-3 lbs. fish
1 green onion
3 large yellow onions, chopped
  in chunks
¼ cup oil
several sprigs of parsley
½ tsp. salt
½ tsp. pepper
2 chili peppers, or 1 tsp. cayenne
  pepper
2 tomatoes, chopped in chunks

For the vegetable stew:

1½ cups vinegar
2 large carrots
2 turnips
½ of a small cauliflower
2 medium tomatoes
1 tsp. salt
1 tsp. pepper
1 chili pepper, crushed, or ½ tsp.
  cayenne pepper
pinch of thyme
2 bay leaves
½ cup dry rice per person,
  cooked

Bake or broil the fish, then flake it into small pieces, removing bones if necessary.

In a blender, food processor or mortar and pestle, grind to a fine paste the onions, oil, parsley, salt and peppers. Add fish and tomatoes and grind again. With oiled hands, shape the paste into tiny balls about the size of large pearls. Set aside.

Combine vinegar with an equal amount of water in a heavy saucepan. Chop the vegetables and add them to the pot along with the salt, peppers and herbs. Bring to a boil; then reduce heat and simmer for 30 minutes. To serve, arrange rice on a platter that has raised edges. Pour on the stew, and scatter fish-paste pearls evenly across the top.

Tiébou Dienn   Senegal

Serves 6-10. This dish, pronounced "cheb-oo jenn," is the national dish of Senegal. It can range from a simple bowl of rice and vegetables to more elaborate combinations of vegetables, spices and sauces.

For the fish and paste:

2 bunches fresh parsley
2-3 green onions
2 large yellow onions
2 tblsp. soy sauce
4-6 cloves garlic
1 tsp. salt
1 heaping tblsp. black pepper
3-4 lbs. thick white fish (1 large fish, if possible)
oil for frying

For the stew and rice:

2-3 onions, finely chopped
3 tblsp. soy sauce
4 oz. tomato paste
4 carrots
4 turnips
1 small cabbage
2 eggplants
5 sweet potatoes
6-8 okra
3-4 chili peppers, or 2 tsp. cayenne pepper
½ cup dry rice per person

In a blender or food processor, purée all the paste ingredients except fish and oil. (Or chop them finely and mash into a paste with a mortar and pestle.) Using a sharp knife, cut deep slits into the fish, but be careful not to cut all the way through. Stuff the purée into the pockets formed by the slits. Heat 2-3 inches of oil in a large, heavy skillet or pot, and carefully fry the fish until it is golden brown. Remove fish from the pot and drain on an absorbent cloth.

Pour off all but a few tablespoons of the oil. Add to the pot the onions, soy sauce and tomato paste, along with about 6 cups water. Chop the vegetables into large chunks, except for the okra, which should be left whole. Stir all the vegetables and pepper into the pot, and cook over moderate heat until tender. For the last couple of minutes of cooking, add the fish.

With a slotted spoon, remove fish and vegetables to a heat-proof container and put in a warm oven. Measure the water left in the pot, pouring some off or adding some, as necessary, for the amount of rice you're cooking (use about 2 cups water per cup of white rice and 2½ cups water per cup of brown). Add the rice and cook; it will be flavored and tinted by the residue of vegetables and spices.

To serve, spread rice in a large bowl, and distribute fish and vegetables evenly across it.

Rougaille of Salted Fish   Mauritius

Serves 4

1 lb. dried salted fish
¼ cup oil
4 onions, chopped
2 sprigs parsley, chopped
6 scallions, chopped
1 cup cherry tomatoes
2 cloves garlic, minced
2 tsp. fresh ginger, grated, or 1
  tsp. ground ginger

Soak fish in cool water for several hours. In a heavy skillet, heat oil to a moderate temperature. Drain fish and pat dry, then fry gently in the oil for 5 or 6 minutes. Add onions, parsley, scallions and tomatoes, and stir frequently until onions are soft and transparent. Then reduce heat, add garlic and ginger, and simmer for 15-20 minutes or until fish is cooked and flavors have blended. Serve with rice.

Kentumere   Ghana

Serves 4. Although higher in fat than many fish, herring is one of the most nutritious and least costly. Because fresh kippered herring tends to be heavily salted as well as smoked, you should soak it before use as you would a dried salt fish. Fillet a fresh kipper by making a slit down the center of the back and carefully pulling out the backbone. Most of the tiny bones should come along with it. For easier preparation, buy kippered herring in cans; it's already filleted and doesn't need soaking. Like palm nut soup, kentumere requires palm oil, carried by certain ethnic and specialty shops.

1 cup palm oil
1 cup onions, coarsely chopped
½ tsp. cayenne pepper
1 cup tomatoes
1 cup kippered herring
4 cups fresh spinach, chopped

Heat the oil in a large skillet or heavy pot, then sauté onions and pepper together. Mash or grind the tomatoes and stir them in, along with the remaining ingredients. Cook at a moderate temperature for 15 minutes, or until fish is tender and flaky. If there is too much oil on the surface for your liking, skim some off with a spoon. Serve kentumere with cooked plantain (see page 111) or rice.

Avocado with Smoked Fish   Ghana

Serves 4 as a first course or 2 as an entrée

½ lb. smoked fish
4 eggs, hard-boiled, with whites
    separated from yolks
¼ cup milk
¼ cup lime juice
¼ tsp. sugar
½ tsp. salt
⅓ cup light cooking oil
2 tblsp. olive oil
2 large ripe avocados
1 large red bell pepper, or a
    dozen pimentos from a can or
    jar

Soak fish in water for several hours. Remove skin and bones, if any, and flake with a fork.

In a deep bowl, mash the egg yolks with the milk until they form a smooth paste. Add sugar, salt, and 1 tablespoon of the lime juice. Then beat in the vegetable oil, a teaspoon or so at a time. Add the olive oil in the same gradual manner. Chop egg whites finely and add them to the bowl, along with the fish. Combine thoroughly but gently.

Just before serving, cut the avocados in half, remove pits, and fill cavities with the fish mixture. Garnish with pepper or pimento.

Poisson de Guinée   Guinea
Guinean Fish

Serves 4-6. Dried shrimp can be bought in Oriental food shops and in the gourmet or spice sections of many supermarkets. If you don't find it pre-ground, you can crush it in a mortar and pestle. Note that you must begin preparations for this dish a day in advance.

For the main dish:

2 bay leaves
2 whole peppercorns
2 cloves
1 cup cooking oil
1 large or 2 small fish (2-3 lbs.)
salt and pepper
1 large onion, chopped
2 large tomatoes, chopped
2 tsp. tomato paste
2 chili peppers or 1 tsp. cayenne
    pepper
1 tblsp. ground dried shrimp
    (optional)
2 cups dry rice, cooked

For the garnish:

1 onion, sliced and separated
    into rings
1 plantain, sliced in rounds
2 tblsp. oil
1 green bell pepper, slivered
2 eggs, hardboiled and sliced

Soak bay leaves, peppercorns and cloves in ⅓ cup of the oil overnight, to flavor it.

The next day, rub fish all over with salt and pepper, and then with the flavored oil. The preferred cooking method is grilling over a charcoal fire. As an alternative, put fish on a rack over a pan to catch drips, and broil in the oven for 6-10 minutes per side, until flesh is tender and flaky.

Meanwhile, make a sauce by heating the remaining oil and frying the onions, tomatoes, tomato paste and hot pepper. After 2 or 3 minutes, add dried shrimp.

In another pan, prepare for the garnish by lightly browning onion rings and plantain pieces in the 2 tblsp. oil. To serve, start by piling the cooked rice on a large platter with raised edges. Lay fish atop the rice and spoon the sauce over it. Garnish with onion rings, plantain pieces, green pepper slivers and egg slices.

Bacalhau Gomes Sa   Angola

Serves 4-6. Salted codfish with potatoes is a favorite in Angola as it is in Portugal.

1-2 lbs. dried salted codfish
3 bay leaves
6 medium potatoes, unpeeled
3 eggs
2 onions, chopped
2 cloves garlic, finely chopped
¼ cup olive oil
pinch of black pepper
¼ tsp. oregano
¼ cup green bell pepper
½ cup parsley, finely chopped
12 olives

Soak the dry salt cod in water overnight. The next day, drain fish and simmer in fresh water, with bay leaves, for 20 minutes. Save the cooking water.

Meanwhile, in separate pots, boil the potatoes and hard-boil the eggs. When potatoes are tender but not mushy, peel them and chop into chunks. Peel and slice the eggs, and set them aside to be used as a garnish.

Using a large, heavy pot or skillet, preferably cast-iron, sauté onions and garlic in moderately hot olive oil, stirring to prevent scorching. Add pepper and oregano. Flake the cod with a fork and mix it in gently, along with the potatoes, green pepper and parsley. Reduce heat and cook for several minutes, stirring to prevent sticking. If the mixture threatens to dry out, moisten with the codfish-cooking water. You may also add more olive oil. (At this point, if your pot is not ovenproof, transfer the mixture to one that is.)

Garnish with olives and egg slices, and heat in a 350° oven until steaming hot.

Lakh-lalo　　　　　　　　　　　　　　　Mali
Fish Stew

Serves 4-6. In Mali, this dish is flavored with a crisp, tart fruit called "netetou." We couldn't come up with an appropriate substitute, but the stew is good without it.

1-2 lbs. dried salted fish
3 large onions, finely chopped
12-16 okra, chopped, or 1 small
　　package frozen okra
4-6 tblsp. olive oil
3 large tomatoes
2 chili peppers or 1 tsp. cayenne
　　pepper

Soak fish in water for several hours. Drain. Then bring 4 cups fresh water to a boil and drop in the fish pieces. Reduce heat and let simmer.

Meanwhile, combine half the onions with the okra and process or pound into a paste. Add them to the fish.

In a separate pot, heat oil to a moderate temperature. Put in remaining onions and sauté until golden brown. Chop the tomatoes and stir them in. (If you want to peel yours, see *About peeling* in the Introduction.) Cover with boiling water, about 1 cup, and add pepper. Reduce heat and simmer.

Cover both pots and let them cook for 45 minutes or so, stirring occasionally. Then uncover the fish and okra mixture and let both pots continue to simmer for another 30-40 minutes, stirring as necessary to prevent sticking. To serve, combine the two mixtures and ladle over stiff porridge (see recipes in *Grains and Bread* chapter).

SEAFOOD

Sauce aux Feuilles de Patates Douces
Burkina Faso
Fish with Sweet Potato Greens

Serves 4-6. If you're a gardener, you can grow your own sweet potato leaves. Otherwise, substitute turnip greens or fresh spinach. You may also use collards or kale, although neither has the same delicate texture as the greenery of sweet potatoes.

This sort of fish sauce, spiced with hot peppers, is common throughout west Africa.

1 lb. dried salted fish
2 small onions, chopped
2 cloves garlic, sliced
2 medium tomatoes
4 tblsp. tomato paste
2 chili peppers or 1 tsp. cayenne pepper
2 tblsp. oil
2-3 cups whole okra
1 lb. sweet potato leaves, or other greens
½ tsp. nutmeg

Soak the fish in water for several hours.

Grind together in a blender or food processor the onions, garlic, tomatoes, tomato paste and hot peppers. (Alternatively, you can crush onions, garlic and peppers with a mortar and pestle, or between two stones. Combine with tomato paste and with tomatoes that have been chopped and mashed with a fork.) In a large, heavy skillet or stew pot, sauté the mixture in moderately hot oil. Stir in okra and enough hot water to cover, about 2 cups. Reduce heat and simmer for 10 minutes.

Meanwhile, in a separate pot, cook greens in boiling water for 10-15 minutes. Drain. Gently add fish, greens and nutmeg to the stew. Simmer for another 45 minutes. Serve with rice or stiff porridge (see recipes in *Grains and Bread* chapter).

97

Sardines in Tomato Sauce   Benin

Serves 2-4

1 large onion, chopped
1 clove garlic, finely chopped
1 tblsp. oil
1 can sardines
2 large tomatoes, chopped, or 2 oz. tomato paste
1 chili pepper, or 1 tsp. cayenne pepper
1 bunch leafy greens, or 1 small package frozen greens (spinach, turnip greens, kale, etc.)

In a large, heavy pan, brown onion and garlic lightly in oil. Add the other ingredients and cover with about 2 cups water. Simmer for 30 minutes. Serve over rice or stiff porridge (see recipes in *Grains and Bread* chapter).

Variations: Substitute fresh, smoked or salt-dried fish for the sardines.

Ingelegde Vis   South Africa
Pickled Fish

Slaves from Dutch territories in the East Indies brought their culinary traditions with them to southern Africa. Although pickled fish no longer play as important a nutritional role as they did in the days before refrigeration, they are still popular. Snoek and hake are commonly used, but any firm, fleshy fish will pickle well. Because these are eaten cold, they make excellent hot weather fare. This recipe serves 4 as a first course or when accompanied by filling side dishes such as potato salad. You must make it 2 days before you plan to eat it.

1 lb. fish
flour for dredging
4 medium onions, sliced
1 cup white vinegar
1 tsp. turmeric
2 tsp. curry powder
1 tsp. peppercorns
2 bay leaves
2 tsp. brown sugar

Pre-heat oven to 350°. Wash and pat dry the fish pieces and dip them in flour to coat. In a baking dish, make a bed of the onion slices and lay fish on top. Combine the remaining ingredients and pour over the fish and onions. Cover with a tight-fitting lid or seal with foil and bake for 1 hour. Remove from the oven and let cool, then refrigerate for 2 days before serving.

Shellfish

Prawns Piripiri
Hot Spiced Prawns

Mozambique

Serves 4-6. Among the abundant shellfish off the coast of Mozambique are the giant shrimp-like crustaceans called prawns. Substitute the largest shrimp you can find for this recipe—less than a dozen per pound. They should be cleaned and shelled, but the tail shell should be left on, if possible, to enhance the flavor.

2-3 lbs. prawns or large shrimp
1 batch piripiri sauce (see
   recipe, page 4)

If you need to clean your own shell-fish, see *About shrimp* in the Introduction.

Make piripiri sauce according to the recipe on page 4. Put prawns or shrimp in a bowl and pour sauce over them, stirring to coat each piece well. Set aside to marinate (soak) for several hours.

Grilling over a charcoal fire is the preferred cooking method; broiling is an alternative. To broil, place whole prawns or shrimp on a rack over a pan that can catch drips. Put the rack about 3 inches from your broiler, and sear for 3-4 minutes on each side. You can also cook them by frying quickly in a skillet of hot butter until they become golden pink. (To avoid scorching and smoking, use clarified butter; see recipe, page 9.)

Meanwhile, heat the marinade in which the prawns or shrimp were soaked. Pass at the table as a sauce. (If you prefer, make a fresh batch of piripiri for serving.)

Camarão de Coco   Mozambique
Coconut Shrimp

Serves 4-6. This shrimp with coconut milk is usually served over rice.

2-3 lbs. shrimp
¼ cup butter or a butter/oil
  mixture
3-4 cloves garlic, minced
1 small onion, finely chopped
2-3 sprigs parsley, finely
  chopped
2 chili peppers, crushed, or 1
  tsp. cayenne pepper
1 tsp. salt
2 tsp. cumin
2 large tomatoes, chopped
2-3 cups coconut milk (see
  recipe, page 7; amount
  depends on how much shrimp
  is used)

If necessary, clean and shell the shrimp (see *About shrimp* in the Introduction). Heat butter in a heavy skillet over moderate heat, and quickly cook the shrimp until they are a rich golden pink. Remove them from the pan with a slotted spoon.

In the same butter, sauté the garlic, onion, parsley and chilies for 2-3 minutes. Add the salt, cumin and tomatoes and cook until the mixture thickens slightly, stirring constantly to avoid burning. Reduce heat to low, return shrimp to the pan and add the coconut milk. Stir until shrimp is heated through.

Akotonshi   Ghana
Stuffed Crabs

Makes 16, to serve 6-8. Look for dried shrimp in Oriental food shops or in the gourmet or spice section of your supermarket.

2 lbs. crab meat
1 tsp. salt
1-inch piece of fresh ginger
4-6 cloves
4 tblsp. cooking oil
1 small onion, minced
1 tsp. ground ginger
2 tomatoes, finely chopped
1 tblsp. tomato paste
2 green bell peppers, finely
    chopped
pinch of paprika
1 tsp. cayenne pepper
1 tblsp. dried shrimp
½ cup whole-wheat bread
    crumbs
1 egg, hard-boiled and finely
    chopped
1 sprig parsley

Put crab meat in boiling salted water along with ginger piece and cloves. Cook about 15 minutes, until meat is tender enough to flake with a fork. Drain, flake and set aside.

In a heavy pot, heat oil to a moderate temperature and add other ingredients in the following sequence, stirring for a minute or so between each: onions, ground ginger, tomatoes, tomato paste, green pepper, paprika, cayenne and dried shrimp. Reduce heat and simmer for 4-5 minutes, stirring constantly, until vegetables are cooked. Add crab meat and stir another couple of minutes to heat it through. Then spoon the mixture into clean crab shells or ramekins (small, individual baking dishes).

Sprinkle bread crumbs on top of each crab and toast under an oven broiler, being careful not to let the crumbs scorch. Garnish with egg and parsley.

Vegetarian Dishes

Vegetable Biryani   # South Africa

Serves 4-6

3 large onions, sliced
4 tblsp. butter, or clarified butter
  (see recipe, page 9)
6 chili peppers, crushed into a
  paste, or 2 tsp. cayenne
  pepper
1 2-inch piece of fresh ginger
10 cloves garlic
½ cup dry lentils, pre-soaked
½ lb. fresh green peas, shelled
½ lb. carrots, chopped
½ lb. green beans, chopped
3 large tomatoes, chopped
6 whole cloves
1 4-inch stick of cinnamon
6 cardamom pods, crushed
1 tsp. turmeric
3 sprigs of fresh mint, or ½ tsp.
  dried mint leaves, pounded
2 cups long-grain white rice
  (Basmati is a good choice),
  uncooked
6 large potatoes, chopped into
  large chunks
1-2 tsp. salt
yogurt

In a large, heavy skillet or stew pot, fry the onions in butter until they are golden brown. With a slotted spoon, remove about ⅓ of the slices and set aside. Add to the pot the ginger, garlic and chili paste, and fry for 5 or 6 minutes, stirring constantly. Then add the lentils, green peas, carrots and green beans. Reduce heat and cook for 15 minutes, adding more butter, or a bit of oil, if necessary.

Add tomatoes, spices and mint, and stir for 5 minutes. Then pour in about a cup of hot water, cover, and simmer until vegetables are about half cooked. Add rice, potatoes, salt, and another 4-5 cups of hot water (use the lesser amount if your vegetables have created quite a bit of liquid). Cover again, and cook for another 20-30 minutes until rice is done and water is absorbed.

To serve, garnish with the reserved onion slices, and pass around a bowl of yogurt as a sauce.

Vegetable Curry   Kenya

Serves 6. Note that the chickpeas need to be pre-cooked, or you may substitute canned ones.

2 large onions, finely chopped
2 tblsp. oil
1 tsp. cumin seeds
1 tsp. mustard seeds (the black kind, if possible)
8 medium potatoes, quartered
1½ tsp. fresh ginger, crushed
1 large garlic clove, minced and crushed
1 tblsp. ground cumin
1 tblsp. whole coriander, crushed
2 chili peppers or 1 tsp. cayenne pepper
½ tsp. turmeric
1 tsp. salt
4 cinnamon sticks
6 cloves
4 oz. tomato paste
½ lb. green beans
½ of a small cauliflower
1 medium eggplant
½ lb. fresh green peas, shelled, or 1 small package frozen green peas
1 bunch of fresh leafy greens (kale, spinach, collards, Swiss chard, etc.), or 1 small package frozen greens
½ cup dry chickpeas, cooked (optional)

Pre-heat oven to 350°.

In a large, heavy skillet or pot, brown onions in moderately hot oil along with the cumin seeds and mustard seeds. Add the potato pieces, peeled or not, as you choose, and stir to coat each piece with the spices. Now add the remaining spices and continue to stir for several minutes.

Thin tomato paste with about ⅔ cup water. Stir into the pot. Add vegetables, one at a time, cooking for a minute or so between each addition, and put in cooked chickpeas last. If your pot is not oven proof, transfer mixture to one that is. Cover with a lid or seal with foil, and bake for about 45 minutes, checking after the first 20 minutes.

The consistency of this curry should be thick, rather than watery, but add more liquid if necessary to prevent burning. Stir occasionally to keep ingredients from sticking to the bottom of the pot. Serve over rice or with Indian bread (see recipes in the *Grains and Bread* chapter).

105

Vegetable Mafé   Senegal

Serves 6-8

2 large onions, finely chopped
4 tblsp. peanut oil
2 cups pumpkin, winter squash, or sweet potatoes, peeled and chopped in chunks
4 turnips
4 medium potatoes, quartered
2 large carrots, chopped in chunks
½ of a small cabbage, coarsely chopped
2 large tomatoes, quartered
1 bunch of fresh leafy greens (spinach, Swiss chard, turnip greens, etc.), or 1 small package frozen greens
2 chili peppers, or 1 tsp. cayenne pepper
2 cups tomato sauce
¾ cup peanut butter

Brown the onions in moderately hot oil in a large, heavy skillet or stew pot. Add the vegetables, one at a time, sautéing each for a minute or so before adding another.

Stir in tomato sauce, along with about a cup of water, reduce heat, and simmer until all the vegetables are tender. Spoon out about half a cup of the hot broth and mix it with the peanut butter to make a smooth paste. Add to the pot, and simmer for another 10-15 minutes. Serve over rice or a stiff porridge (see recipes in the *Grains and Bread* chapter).

Grilled Plantain   Togo

Serves 4-6. Plantains cooked this way are a popular street food that are also good with nearly any meal.

4 plantains
¼ tsp. cayenne pepper

Sprinkle plantains with pepper, and grill until tender over a charcoal fire. Or you may broil them for 6-8 minutes about 4 inches from your oven's heating coils. Serve hot.

Futari   Tanzania
Coconut-Peanut Pumpkin

Serves 6-8. What could be better than the fragrant blending of coconut, citrus, cinnamon and cloves? You may substitute winter squash for the pumpkin.

2 cups pumpkin, peeled and cut
   into 2-inch chunks
2 cups sweet potatoes, peeled
   and chopped into 2-inch
   chunks
3 tblsp. onion, finely chopped
1 tblsp. butter
juice of ½ a lemon
½ tsp. cloves
1 tsp. salt
1-2 cups coconut milk (see
   recipe, page 7)
1 tsp. cinnamon

If your pumpkin or winter squash is very tough and hard to cut, you may want to estimate the amount you will need, and then use a very sharp knife to cut off a big chunk. Boil the piece for 3-4 minutes, then plunge into cold water until cool enough to handle. At this point, the pumpkin or squash will be easier to peel and chop.

Fry the onion in butter until just golden brown. Combine with the pumpkin or squash and the sweet potatoes in a heavy pot. Add lemon juice, cloves, salt and a cup of coconut milk. Cover and simmer for 10-12 minutes.

Uncover, stir gently and add cinnamon. Cook for another 15-20 minutes until vegetables are tender, stirring constantly to prevent sticking. Add more coconut milk or a bit of water if mixture becomes dry.

Variation: Thin ¼ cup peanut butter with ½ cup hot water, adding water a couple of spoonsful at a time. Then add more water to make a cup, and use in the recipe instead of coconut milk.

Eggplant Curry   Tanzania

Serves 6

4 large eggplants, peeled and
    chopped in chunks
2 tsp. salt
2 large onions, finely chopped
2 cloves garlic, sliced and
    crushed
4 tblsp. oil
1 tsp. cumin seed, crushed
1 tsp. ground coriander
3 cardamom pods
2 tsp. fresh ginger, grated
½ tsp. turmeric
1 tsp. salt
2 chili peppers, crushed, or 1
    tsp. cayenne pepper
2-3 large potatoes, chopped in
    chunks
1 tomato, peeled (see *About
    peeling* in the Introduction),
    and finely chopped
1 tsp. tomato paste

Sprinkle 1 teaspoon of the salt over the eggplant pieces, stir, and let sit for 6-8 minutes. Meanwhile, in a large, heavy skillet or stew pot, sauté onions and garlic in moderately hot oil until golden brown, stirring and watching carefully to prevent scorching. Add all the spices and the pepper, and continue to stir for another couple of minutes.

Squeeze eggplant pieces between your fingers, or press them firmly with a fork, to squeeze out excess moisture. Then gather them into a clean, lint-free cloth and gently squeeze again. Dump pieces into the pot. Stir until eggplant becomes limp and slightly golden, adding a bit more oil if necessary. Then add potatoes and let them brown on all sides.

When potatoes are somewhat tender, but still resistant to a fork, add tomatoes, tomato sauce and 1½ cups of water. Stir, bring to a boil, then reduce heat and simmer until vegetables are tender but not mushy. The sauce should be thick, like syrup, rather than watery. If it isn't, simmer a little longer, stirring as necessary to prevent sticking. If it's too thick, add more water. Serve over rice.

Coconut Corn Curry   East Africa

Serves 4-6

4 cups fresh or frozen corn
   kernels
3 tblsp. poppy seeds
1 tsp. cumin seeds
1 tsp. coriander seeds
1 tsp. sesame seeds
1 tblsp. fresh ginger, grated
2 chili peppers, or 1 tsp. cayenne
   pepper
meat from ½ of a fresh coconut,
   grated (see pages 6 and 7), or
   ¾ cup packaged, shredded
   coconut (unsweetened)
½ cup peanuts
3 tblsp. butter or clarified butter
   (see recipe, page 9)
1 tsp. salt
5-6 cups coconut milk (see
   recipe, page 7)

Cook the corn by boiling in a small amount of water until tender. Drain and set aside.

Using a mortar and pestle, blender or food processor, grind all the spices, the coconut meat and the peanuts into a smooth paste. In a large, heavy skillet or stew pot, heat the butter and fry the paste for 4 or 5 minutes, stirring constantly. Add the corn, salt and coconut milk, reduce heat, and simmer until the sauce becomes fairly thick, about 10-15 minutes. Stir occasionally to prevent sticking. Serve over rice.

Zucchini with Peanuts   Chad

Serves 4-6. The use of zucchini in this recipe reflects a French influence.

4 small zucchini squash
½ tsp. salt
2 tblsp. butter or oil
1 cup unsalted peanuts, raw or
   roasted, coarsely ground

Simmer whole squash in about half a cup of salted water until very tender, 10-12 minutes. Combine squash and butter, and process or mash to a smooth consistency. Top with nuts.

Variation: When zucchini is tender, drain and slice it, gently stir in butter, and top with nuts.

109

Yataklete Kilkil

Ethiopia

Spiced Vegetables

Serves 6

1½ lbs. new potatoes
1 broccoli head, including stem
4-5 large carrots, sliced in
  rounds
1 small cauliflower, coarsely
  chopped
1 medium-size onion, finely
  chopped
½ cup niter kebbeh (see recipe,
  page 9)

If your new potatoes are very small, leave them whole. If not, halve or quarter them. Cut stem off broccoli, remove the tough outer fiber, and chop inner stem coarsely. Also chop the broccoli head.

Steam, over boiling water, the potatoes, broccoli stem, carrots and cauliflower. After 10 minutes, add broccoli. Continue to steam another few minutes until vegetables are just tender when pierced with a fork.

Meanwhile, in a large, heavy skillet or stew pot, sauté the onions in half the niter kebbeh until they are transparent. Mix in the steamed vegetables, except the broccoli. Cover and cook for 6-8 minutes, stirring frequently. Add broccoli, and cook for another 4 or 5 minutes. Heat the remaining niter kebbeh to pass around at the table. Serve yataklete kilkil with injera (see recipe in *Grains and Bread* chapter) or over rice.

Yam Balls   West Africa

Serves 6-8. West African yams are starchier and more fibrous than what North Americans call yams. For different effects, try this recipe with either white potatoes or sweet potatoes.

4 cups yams, cooked
1 large onion, finely chopped
3 medium-size tomatoes, peeled (see *About peeling* in the Introduction), and finely chopped
1 tsp. cayenne pepper
2 cups peanut oil
½ tsp. dried thyme
½ tsp. salt
2 eggs, beaten
flour

Mash or process the cooked yams until smooth. Set aside.

Fry half the onions and half the tomatoes in ¼ cup of the oil until onions are limp. Add thyme and salt and mix well.

Scrape the mixture into a bowl, dump in the remaining onions and tomatoes, and the yams. Mix well and beat in the eggs. Turn the mixture out onto a floured surface. With greased hands, shape spheres about the size of golf balls. Heat the remaining oil to a temperature of between 350° and 375° (see *About frying* in the Introduction), and fry balls until they are golden brown all around—about 4 or 5 minutes each. Drain on clean, absorbent cloths and serve immediately.

Boiled Plantain   Burundi

Serves 4. Boiled plantains make an easy-to-prepare base for meat or vegetable stews. Because of the amount of agricultural chemicals used in fruit cultivation, we suggest a good soap and hot-water scrub before cooking plantains this way. If you prefer, you may peel them before boiling.

4 large plantains

Drop unpeeled plantains in boiling water. Cook for 15-20 minutes until a test plantain is tender when pierced with a fork. Peel before serving.

111

Sweet Potato Puffs   Liberia

Serves 4. Note that the sweet potatoes must be cooked, mashed and chilled before you can prepare the puffs.

1-2 cups flour
1½ tsp. baking powder
½ tsp. salt
¼ tsp. ground cloves
¼ tsp. cinnamon
¼ tsp. nutmeg
2 eggs, slightly beaten
2 cups sweet potatoes, mashed
   and chilled
oil for deep frying

Sift together the flour, baking powder and spices. In another bowl, combine the eggs and potatoes, then beat in the dry-ingredient mixture to make a stiff dough.

Roll the dough out on a lightly floured surface to a thickness of about a half inch. With a knife, cookie cutters, or the rim of a glass, cut into shapes. Fry in deep fat (see *About frying* in the Introduction) for 2 or 3 minutes. Drain on clean, absorbent cloths.

Variation: Sprinkle with confectioners' sugar and serve as a dessert.

Fried Cabbage   Tanzania

Serves 6-8

1 small onion, finely chopped
6 tblsp. oil
1 large tomato, sliced
½ tsp. salt
½ tsp. curry powder
1 medium-size cabbage, thinly
   shredded
2 carrots, sliced into rounds
1 green bell pepper, chopped

Over moderate heat, fry the onion in oil until lightly browned, stirring to prevent scorching. Add tomatoes, salt and curry powder and continue stirring for 2 or 3 minutes.

Add cabbage, carrots and pepper, and mix well. Then pour in about half a cup of water. Cover the pot, reduce heat, and simmer until liquid is absorbed and cabbage is still slightly crunchy.

Potato Balls   Tanzania

Makes several dozen balls. Serve as a side dish or snack. Look for chickpea flour, sometimes called "gram" flour, in Indian food shops.

3 cups potatoes, peeled and
  chopped
¼ cup lime juice
½ tsp. salt
1 chili pepper, crushed, or ½ tsp.
  cayenne pepper
1 cup chickpea flour
coconut oil
½ cup of fresh coconut meat,
  grated (see page 6)

Boil potatoes until soft. Drain, combine with lime juice, salt and pepper, and grind or process to a smooth batter. With greased hands, shape the batter into 1-inch balls and roll the balls in flour.

Make a condiment to pass around with the balls by mixing coconut and pepper with 2 or 3 tablespoons of water. Set aside.

In a heavy skillet or pot, heat oil to about 375° (see *About frying* in the Introduction), and fry the balls a few at a time. Drain on clean, absorbent cloths, and serve hot. Pass around the coconut/pepper mixture for individuals to serve themselves.

Baked Cabbage with Tomatoes   Morocco

Serves 4

1 medium-size cabbage
3 large tomatoes, peeled (see
  About peeling in the Introduction), and chopped
½ tsp. garlic powder
1 small onion, chopped
¼ tsp. salt
¼ tsp. pepper
⅛ tsp. cumin

Pre-heat oven to 350°.

Quarter the cabbage and boil it for 5 minutes. Drain, and put the pieces into a baking dish. Combine remaining ingredients, pour them over the cabbage, and bake for about 20 minutes.

113

Sweet and Sour Carrots   Morocco

Serves 4-6

3-4 medium-size carrots
¼ cup onion, minced
½ tsp. ground nutmeg
6 tblsp. butter
2 tblsp. white vinegar
½ cup seedless raisins
2 tblsp. brown sugar

Scrape the carrots and slice them into ¼-inch thick rounds. Melt butter in a heavy saucepan and add carrots, onions and nutmeg. When onions are lightly browned, pour in vinegar. Cook, covered, over low heat until carrots are tender.

Meanwhile, soak raisins in ½ cup warm water. When carrots are done, drain raisins and dump them into the saucepan along with the brown sugar. Stir gently until raisins are heated through. Serve steaming hot.

Okra and Greens   Gabon

Serves 4-6. Much Gabonese food is fiery-hot. Although we've reduced the pepper, you may want to further curtail it. You may use any edible, dark, leafy greens, but turnip greens and collards are particularly tasty when combined with okra. Try substituting pine nuts for palm nuts.

1 small onion, finely chopped
2 tblsp. palm oil, or other cooking oil
1 lb. greens, shredded
16 okra
½ cup palm nuts
4 chili peppers, finely chopped
  and crushed, or 2 tsp. cayenne
  pepper

In a large, heavy saucepan, sauté onions in oil until golden brown. Add remaining ingredients plus about ¼ cup water. Simmer over low heat, covered, until nuts and greens are tender, about 20 minutes.

Masamba   Malawi
Greens

Serves 4-6. This recipe may be prepared with such leafy greens as kale, spinach, collards or sweet potato leaves. Pumpkin leaves are especially sweet and delicious, but you will need more of them than you might imagine, as they cook down significantly. The secret of this dish's flavor is the groundnut powder, made by grinding raw or roasted peanuts in a blender or food processor until fine and powdery. Or you can pound them in a mortar and pestle or grind them between two stones.

1 lb. greens, finely chopped
½ tsp. salt
4 medium-size tomatoes, chopped
4 tblsp. groundnut powder
2 small onions, finely chopped (optional)

Put greens in just enough boiling salted water to cover. Cook over medium heat until soft, adding more water as needed to keep them from sticking. After a minute or so, lay the tomatoes and peanut powder on top of the greens, but do not stir. If you're using onions, place them on top as well. Reduce heat and simmer for 15 minutes. Stir, then simmer an additional 15 minutes. Eat with nsima or other stiff porridge (see recipes in *Grains and Bread* chapter).

Plantains in Coconut Milk   Kenya

Serves 4-6. Try these with curries or with fish.

3-4 plantains, sliced in rounds
¼ tsp. salt
1 tsp. curry powder
½ tsp. cinnamon
⅛ tsp. cloves
1-2 cups coconut milk (see recipe, page 7)

Combine all ingredients except coconut milk in a heavy saucepan. Pour in 1 cup of coconut milk and simmer over low heat until plantain is very tender and milk is absorbed. Add more coconut milk if necessary. Serve hot.

Yegomen Kitfo   Ethiopia
Collards with Spiced Cottage Cheese

Serves 6-8

For the cottage cheese:

12 oz. cottage cheese
1/3 cup niter kebbeh (see recipe,
  page 9)
2 garlic cloves, slightly crushed
1/4 tsp. ground cardamom
1/2 tsp. salt
1/4 tsp. pepper

For the greens:

2 lbs. collards, chopped
2 tblsp. chili pepper, finely
  chopped
1 tblsp. fresh ginger, grated
1 tsp. garlic, finely chopped
1/2 tsp. ground cardamom
1/4 cup niter kebbeh
2 tblsp. onion, finely chopped

Mix the first group of ingredients together and let the flavors combine at room temperature for 15 minutes. Take out the garlic cloves.

In several tablespoons of water, steam collards for about 20 minutes. Add the rest of the second group of ingredients and mix thoroughly.

Serve collards and cottage cheese mixture in separate dishes, or spoon greens over cottage cheese in one large bowl.

Spinach Stew Central African Republic

Serves 6

2 small onions, finely chopped
2 tblsp. oil
2 tomatoes, peeled (see *About
    peeling* in the Introduction),
    and sliced
1 green bell pepper, chopped
2 lbs. fresh spinach, chopped, or
    2 small packages frozen
    spinach
1 tsp. salt
2 chili peppers, or ½ tsp. cayenne
    pepper
4 tblsp. peanut butter

In a heavy skillet or stew pot, sauté onions in moderately hot oil until golden. Stir in tomatoes and green pepper. After a minute or so, add spinach, salt and hot pepper. Cover, reduce heat, and simmer for 5 minutes.

Thin peanut butter with several tablespoons of warm water to make a smooth paste. Add to the pot. Continue cooking for another 10-15 minutes, stirring frequently, and keeping a close watch to prevent burning. Add small amounts of water as necessary so that the stew doesn't stick to the pot bottom. Serve with rice or a stiff porridge (see recipes in *Grains and Bread* chapter).

UM'Bido South Africa
Greens and Peanuts

Serves 6.

2 lbs. cooked fresh spinach or
    pumpkin leaves, or 4 small
    packages frozen spinach
1 cup peanuts, coarsely ground
2 tblsp. butter
½ tsp. salt
¼ tsp. pepper

Cook fresh spinach in enough boiling water to cover. Frozen spinach should be cooked in ½ cup water, or less. After 4 or 5 minutes, sprinkle in the peanuts and stir well. Continue cooking over medium heat for about 30 minutes, adding more water if necessary to prevent burning. Just before serving, drain and mix in the butter, salt and pepper.

Legumes

Before trying the recipes in this section, please read *About grains* in the Introduction. The group of beans and peas called "legumes" or "pulses," provide valuable protein as well as diversity to a vegetarian diet. When complemented with corn or whole grains, they offer complete protein. They also make excellent, filling accompaniments to meat dishes.

Because their cooking times can vary widely, it is often convenient to pre-cook and freeze them for quick use. When you're very pressed for time, you can substitute canned beans or peas for dried ones.

Except for the lentils, which are treated as side dishes, the estimate of how many people each recipe will serve is based on the assumption that it will be a main feature of the meal. So you should reduce amounts accordingly if you plan to serve them alongside another entree.

Beans with Coconut Milk   Tanzania

Serves 6-8. This version of beans in coconut milk is from the spice island of Zanzibar.

2 cups dried beans or chickpeas,
   pre-soaked
1½ cups coconut milk (see
   recipe, page 7)
1 medium-size tomato, chopped
2-4 whole cloves, crushed
1 clove garlic, minced and
   crushed
1½ tsp. turmeric

Cook beans in enough water to cover until you estimate that they are about half done. Drain the beans, then add to the pot the coconut milk, tomato and spices. Continue to boil until beans are tender. Serve hot with rice.

Maharagwe   Kenya
Spiced Red Beans in Coconut Milk

Serves 4-6

1 cup dried red kidney beans
2 medium-size yellow onions,
    chopped
1-2 tblsp. oil
2-3 tomatoes, chopped
1 tsp. salt
2 tsp. turmeric
3 chili peppers, ground into a
    paste, or 1½ tsp. cayenne
    pepper
2 cups coconut milk (see recipe,
    page 7)

In a large pot, cover the beans with water and simmer until they are just tender. Sauté onions in oil until golden brown. Add, with the remaining ingredients, to the pot, and simmer another several minutes until beans are very tender and tomatoes are cooked. Serve over rice or a stiff porridge (see recipes in the *Grains and Bread* chapter).

Beans with Shredded Coconut   Tanzania

Serves 6-8. Coconut and spice-flavored vegetables are a common feature of recipes from Tanzania's off shore islands of Zanzibar and Pemba.

2 cups dried beans or chickpeas,
    pre-soaked
2 cups potatoes, diced
3 cloves garlic, chopped
½ cup coconut oil, or other oil
1 tblsp. cumin
1 tblsp. coriander
juice of 1 lime (or more, to taste)
1 cup fresh coconut meat,
    grated (see page 6)
2 tsp. turmeric
½ tsp. salt
2 chili peppers, or 1 tsp. cayenne
    pepper

Cook the beans in enough water to cover until tender. Drain. At the same time, cook potatoes until they are just tender. Drain those as well.

Meanwhile, fry garlic in the coconut oil. When it is golden brown, add the remaining ingredients along with the cooked beans and potatoes. Serve hot with rice.

Oshingali
Black-eyed Peas
Serves 4.

Namibia

4 cups fresh black-eyed peas
1 tsp. salt
1 chili pepper, crushed or ½ tsp.
  cayenne pepper

Soak fresh peas in cold water for about 5 minutes to soften. Using both hands, rub and gently squeeze the peas as they continue to soak. This process will gradually loosen the skins, which will float to the top and should be skimmed off and discarded.

Drain and rinse the peas, add salt and hot pepper, and cover with clean water. Boil until tender. Serve, along with the cooking water, over oshifima or another stiff porridge (see recipes in the *Grains and Bread* chapter).

Pinto Beans with Potatoes

Rwanda

Serves 6-8. This dish traditionally is made with manioc (also known as cassava), but potatoes are a reasonable substitute.

2 cups dried pinto beans,
  pre-soaked
3 large potatoes, chopped
2 celery stalks, chopped
1 tsp. salt
1 onion, thinly sliced
4 tblsp. peanut oil

Cover the pinto beans with water, bring to a boil, then reduce heat and simmer until beans are just tender. Add the potato chunks, celery and salt, along with more water if necessary to cover. Continue to cook over low heat.

Just before the potatoes and beans are tender, gently fry the onion in oil in a large, heavy skillet or stew pot. Using a slotted spoon, add the beans and potatoes to the pot, and stir until well mixed and heated through. Serve hot over rice or a stiff porridge (see recipes in *Grains and Bread* chapter).

Spiced Lentils   Morocco

Serves 6-8. Fresh coriander can often be found at Latin or Oriental markets, where it is called, respectively, "cilantro" or "Chinese parsley." If you can't find any, substitute parsley. These lentils are a good accompaniment to brochettes (see recipe, page 74).

2 cups dark lentils
1 onion, finely chopped
½ tsp. turmeric
1 tsp. salt
2 large onions, thinly sliced
2 tblsp. butter
2 tomatoes, peeled (see *About peeling* in the Introduction), and chopped
5 cloves garlic, crushed
1 tsp. ground cumin
¼ tsp. black pepper
1 tsp. ground ginger
½ tsp. chili pepper, or ¼ tsp. cayenne pepper
2 tblsp. fresh coriander, chopped

Soak lentils for 2 hours in cold water. Drain. Then simmer them in enough water to cover plus 1 inch, along with the chopped onion, turmeric and salt. Cook about 1½-2 hours until lentils are tender, adding a bit more water if necessary to prevent them from drying out and sticking.

When lentils are nearly done, sauté the sliced onion in the butter in a large skillet. Add the remaining ingredients (not including those in the lentil pot). Cook over low heat for 5 or 6 minutes. Then stir in the contents of the lentil pot. Add coriander and simmer another 10 minutes to blend flavors, stirring several times. Serve hot.

Vegetarian Lentils   South Africa

Serves 6-8. These lentils are a good complement to any kind of curry.

2 cups orange lentils
1 tsp. salt
¼ cup oil
1 large onion, chopped
1 tsp. fresh ginger, grated and
    crushed
1 tsp. garlic, crushed
1 tsp. ground coriander
1 tsp. turmeric
1 tsp. cumin seeds, pounded
1 tsp. cardamom seeds, pounded
1 tsp. chili pepper, or ½ tsp.
    cayenne pepper
¼ cup tomatoes, peeled (option-
    al, see *About peeling* in the
    Introduction), and chopped

Dissolve salt in enough boiling water to cover the lentils. Add lentils and cook until tender. Drain, then mash slightly with a fork or potato masher.

Heat the oil to a moderate temperature in a large skillet, and fry onions until golden. Add remaining ingredients (not including lentils). Simmer for a few minutes, then add lentils, stirring well. Heat until the mixture is quite thick. Serve hot.

Dess b'l-besla   Algeria
Lentils with Onions

Serves 6-8

2 cups dried lentils, pre-soaked
2 cloves garlic, minced
pinch of cinnamon
½ tsp. cumin
pinch of black pepper
1 chili pepper, or ½ tsp. cayenne
    pepper
½ tsp. salt
2 large onions, thinly sliced
3 tblsp. olive oil
3-4 bay leaves

Bring the lentils to a boil in enough water to cover them. At the same time, make a spice paste by crushing together the garlic, cinnamon, cumin, peppers and salt, along with 2 teaspoons of water.

After 2 or 3 minutes, drain lentils thoroughly and transfer to another pot. Add the spice paste, followed by the onions, oil and bay leaves. Stir over moderate heat for several minutes, then once again add water to cover. Reduce heat, cover the pot, and simmer until lentils are tender. Uncover for a few minutes before removing pot from the heat so that liquid may thicken a bit.

Bananas with Green Split Peas   Rwanda

Serves 6-8

2 cups dried green split peas,
  pre-soaked
4 ripe bananas
½ tsp. salt
2 tblsp. palm oil, or other cooking oil
1 very small onion, thinly sliced

Cook the peas in enough water to cover until tender, about 1½ hours. Peel bananas and lay them whole on top of the peas without mixing. Continue to cook for about 10 minutes until bananas are soft, adding a bit of water if necessary to prevent peas from sticking to the bottom of the pot.

Meanwhile, heat the palm oil in a skillet or pot large enough to hold the peas and bananas. Brown the onions. Then, with a slotted spoon, remove bananas and peas from the first pot and add to the onions. Sprinkle in the salt and continue to cook over medium heat, stirring gently but constantly, until oil has been absorbed. Serve hot.

Fule

Sudan

Fava Bean Spread

Serves 4-6. Fava beans, or European broad beans, are a staple food in much of the Arab world, but to a small percentage of people they may be toxic. If you are of Middle Eastern ancestry, and have never eaten fava beans before, you might want to check with your doctor before trying this recipe.

4 cups fava beans, cooked (you may use canned beans, with good results)
2 large tomatoes, very ripe, finely chopped
2 medium-size red onions, minced
¼ lb. feta cheese (optional)
1 tsp. cumin
½ tsp. salt
½ tsp. black pepper
juice of 2 lemons
¼ cup oil
4-6 pieces pita bread

Combine beans with the other ingredients. Mash thoroughly, or whirl to a paste in a blender or food processor. Put into a pot to re-heat quickly, then fill pita bread pockets with the mixture. Serve immediately.

Grains and Bread

Baking at home is not a common cooking method in Africa, except in those areas where European influences are prevalent. Even in Morocco, where freshly-baked bread is regarded as almost sacred, the family's daily supply is mixed at home, then sent to a communal oven for baking.

But as is true everywhere in the world, the growth of an urban middle class changes cultural patterns. In Africa, one result is that more people have their own ovens. Still, for most of the African continent, the staple food is rice or a stiff porridge. In places as far apart as Madagascar and northern Nigeria, rice is eaten two or three times a day. From South Africa to Ghana, corn flour or cassava becomes a firm, pliable mass used to scoop up soups and stews.

For all of their importance, though, the porridges generally are bland and unassuming. They function as the neutral base upon which the flavors of sauces and stews can stand alone.

This chapter offers a selection of grains and breads and porridges from around the continent.

Ujeqe   South Africa
Dumpling

Serves 4

1½ cups whole wheat flour
1 cup cornmeal
2 tsp. baking powder
pinch of salt
1½ tblsp. butter
milk
2 eggs

In a large bowl, sift dry ingredients together. Beat eggs into 1 cup milk, and stir gradually into the dry mixture. Add enough additional milk to make a stiff dough that doesn't stick to the sides of the bowl.

With damp hands, shape dough into a semi-flat circle, and place into a greased steamer. Steam until cooked through, about 45 minutes. Like a loaf of bread, dumpling is done when a knife stuck into the center comes out clean.

Ksra   Morocco
Moroccan Bread

Makes 2 8-inch diameter loaves. In Morocco, ksra is usually a sour-dough bread, but this version substitutes yeast. Use a mixture of whole wheat, barley and unbleached flours in any proportions you like, until you settle on a blend that you prefer.

2 tsp. sugar
2 tblsp. active dry yeast (2 packets)
7-8 cups flour
2 tsp. salt
2 tblsp. butter, melted, or clarified butter (see recipe, page 9)
¾ cup milk, room temperature or slightly warmed
1 tsp. caraway seeds (optional)
1 tsp. aniseed (optional)
¼ cup corn meal

In a bowl or measuring cup that will hold at least 2 cups, dissolve sugar in 1 cup of lukewarm water. (Test the water temperature as you would a baby's bottle—it's right when a few drops of it placed on the inside of your wrist feel slightly warm.) Then stir in the yeast until it, too, dissolves. Set mixture in a warm place for about 5 minutes until bubbly and nearly double in volume.

Meanwhile, combine 7 cups flour and the salt in a large bowl. When yeast mixture is ready, stir it into the flour, along with the milk. While beating with a wooden spoon, or mixing with your hand, gradually add enough water to form a stiff dough. Start with 1 cup (although the amount needed can vary widely). If necessary, add more flour. When you have a dough that holds together and pulls away from the side of the bowl, turn it out onto a floured surface. Let it "rest" for 10-15 minutes.

Knead by flattening the ball of dough with the heels of your hands, while pushing away from you, and then folding up the edges and pushing down again. Repeat this process until dough is smooth and elastic, 15-20 minutes for a good chewy loaf. If you're using caraway or aniseed, add them during the last stages of kneading.

Divide the dough into 2 equal parts, and put them one at a time into a greased bowl. Turn each over once to lightly grease all sides. Then, form the dough into two round, slightly dome-shaped loaves about 2 inches thick in the center. Sprinkle with corn meal, place on a baking sheet that also has been sprinkled with corn meal, cover with a lint-free cloth, and set in a warm place to rise for about an hour. (If you don't have a place that is between 75°

and 85°, it may take longer for your dough to rise, and the texture of your bread will be a bit coarser—which you may prefer.)

While bread is rising, pre-heat oven to 400°. When rising is complete, prick the loaves with a fork in decorative patterns. Bake for 20 minutes, then lower heat to 300° and bake for another 40-50 minutes, or until bread is golden and small cracks form in the crust.

Puris   South Africa
Indian Crispbread

Serves 4-6. These light, puffy breads usually are eaten with curries, but are also good as snacks. They aren't difficult to make, but before starting you should read About frying *in the Introduction.*

4 cups whole wheat flour
2½ tblsp. butter
oil for deep frying

Put flour in a large bowl and have butter ready. Chill your fingers by running them under cold water or rubbing them with ice. Dry well. Then, with you fingertips, mix butter into the flour by rubbing bits of flour and butter briskly in small circles until butter is well distributed throughout the flour.

Stirring constantly with a wooden spoon, gradually add enough water to make a stiff dough, as with loaf bread. The dough is moist enough when it begins to hold together and pull away from the side of the bowl.

Turn the dough ball out onto a lightly greased surface. Pinch off small portions one at a time and roll them into circles about ⅛-inch thick and 4-5 inches in diameter. Heat the oil to a temperature of 350° to 375°, or until test piece of dough browns and floats to the top.

With practice, you can fry 2 or 3 puris at a time, but start with one. Gently slide it into the hot oil. It will sink, then float to the top. When it does, press it gently with the back of a slotted spoon to make it puff. Turn it over and let it cook another minute until just golden brown. With the slotted spoon, lift out the cooked bread and lay it on clean, absorbent cloths to drain. Continue in the same way until all the dough is used. Serve hot.

Roti   South Africa
Indian Flatbread

Makes 4 8-inch circles. Strictly speaking, these are creations of the East Indies, "roti" being the Malay word for bread. They are meant to be eaten with curries.

1 cup unbleached flour
1 cup whole wheat flour
¼ tsp. salt
¼ cup clarified butter (see recipe, page 9), or butter, melted
¼ cup milk, room temperature
oil for skillet

Combine flours with salt.

In a large bowl, mix milk with ¾ cup of warm water. Add 1 tablespoon of the butter, and gradually begin adding flour. Blend well to make a soft dough, adding more flour or water as necessary. The consistency should be a little less firm than loaf-bread dough.

Cover bowl with a lint-free cloth and let the dough "rest" for about an hour. Then turn it out onto a floured surface and divide into 4 equal parts. To prepare each, roll out into a circle about 8 inches across and brush with butter. Fold in half, brush top with more butter, and fold in half again. Then roll out into a circle about ⅛-inch thick.

Transfer dough to a large, hot skillet or griddle, lightly brushed with oil. Turn several times, cooking until the roti is cooked through and surfaces are flecked with brown. Brush each side with butter a final time, and sit in a warm spot while you cook remaining roti.

Variation: For less richness, substitute a polyunsaturated oil for the butter, leaving out entirely the final brushing of the cooked roti.

Injera

Ethiopia

Flat Bread

Serves 6-8. These are the flat, airy, slightly fermented round breads that are an indispensable accompaniment to Ethiopian wats (see recipe for doro wat, page 40). Made of teff, a member of the millet family, they are light in color, slightly spongy in texture, and pliable enough to drape over the edge of a platter. Making them properly is a 2 or 3-day process, but Lonna Harkrader has developed this imitation that has been pronounced excellent by a number of Ethiopians.

4 cups self-rising flour
1 cup whole wheat flour
1 tsp. baking powder
2 cups club soda

Combine flours and baking powder in a bowl. Add club soda plus about 4 cups water. Mix into a smooth, fairly thin batter.

Heat a large, non-stick skillet. When a drop of water bounces on the pan's surface, dip enough batter from the bowl to cover the bottom of the skillet, and pour it in quickly, all at once. Swirl the pan so that the entire bottom is evenly coated, then set it back on the heat.

When the moisture has evaporated and small holes appear on the surface, remove the injera. It should be cooked on only one side, and not browned. If your first try is too pasty and undercooked, you may need to cook it a little longer or to make the next one thinner. But, as with French crêpes, be careful not to cook them too long, or you'll have a crisp bread that may be tasty but won't fold around bits of stew.

Stack the injera one on top of the other as you cook, covering with a clean cloth to prevent their drying out. To serve, lay them on a platter in overlapping concentric circles, beginning with the inside and moving outwards until edges of the outer ring fall over the edge.

131

Couscous   North-West Africa

There are several ways of steaming and softening this form of semolina wheat that is a base for north African stews. The preferred method is to use a couscousière. If you have one, we'll assume you know how to use it. If you don't have one, here's how to proceed.

Get dry couscous grain in an ethnic or gourmet grocery or a natural foods store. Allow 2 oz. per person for a meal.

Pour the couscous into a large bowl and cover it with cold water. Stir, and let it sit for about 10 minutes. Then scrape the damp grain out onto a clean absorbent cloth such as a linen dish towel. (If all the water hasn't been soaked up, you should drain it off first.) Leave the grain to swell for 15 minutes. If you prefer, you can leave the grains in the bowl, but as they are more confined, they may not become quite as fluffy.

Now you must find a way to steam the couscous. A colander that will sit part way down into a pot, without sinking to the bottom, can become a homemade couscousière. But if your colander, like most, has holes too large to prevent the couscous grains from falling through, you must line it with a clean, porous cloth. When everything is ready, bring water in the pot to a boil, and steam the couscous, uncovered, for 20 minutes.

Now the couscous must swell and steam a second time, but with slight variations. Once again, put it into a bowl or onto the towel. Sprinkle cold water over it—perhaps half a cup for every pound of couscous—and rub grains between your fingers to break up any lumps that have formed. After it has sat for 10 minutes, rub some oil onto your hands and rework the grains with your fingers. (For special occasions, use butter to grease and separate the grains.)

Finally, steam the couscous for 25 more minutes, and serve hot.

There is nothing complicated about this process, but it does take some time. If it sounds too ambitious, try the packaged, pre-cooked grain that is widely available where couscous is sold, and follow the simple directions on the box. True connoisseurs argue, no doubt correctly, that you will never know what *real* couscous tastes like unless you steam your own. We must confess, though, that we have resorted to the "instant" kind often and found it acceptable.

Fufu   Ghana

Serves 6-8. Conventional west African fufu is made by boiling such starchy foods as cassava, yam, plantain or rice, then pounding them into a glutenous mass, usually in a giant, wooden mortar and pestle. The first early-morning sounds of rural west Africa are often the rhythmic thud-thud's of fufu being made. This adaptation for North Americans may trouble you if you try to stick to minimally-processed foods. But it's worth trying at least once with west African groundnut stews (see recipes, pages 42-44).

2½ cups Bisquick
2½ cups instant potato flakes

Bring 6 cups of water to a rapid boil in a large, heavy pot. Combine the two ingredients and add to the water.

Stir constantly for 10-15 minutes—a process that needs two people for best results: one to hold the pot while the other stirs vigorously with a strong implement (such as a thick wooden spoon). The mixture will become very thick and difficult to stir, but unless you are both vigilant and energetic, you'll get a lumpy mess.

When the fufu is ready (or you've stirred to the limits of your endurance!), dump about a cup of the mixture into a wet bowl and shake until it forms itself into a smooth ball. Serve on a large platter alongside a soup or stew.

Bidia   Zaire
Stiff Porridge

Serves 4-6. This recipe from the Kasai area of Zaire is one version of what is called "nsima" in Malawi and Zambia, "ugali" in Kenya and Tanzania, "oshi-fima" in Namibia, and "mealie-meal" or "putu" among English or Zulu-speaking South Africans. It may be made with just water instead of milk, or with equal parts tapioca flour and cornmeal instead of with cornmeal alone.

1¼ cups white cornmeal ~Coarse!
1 cup milk

Heat a cup of water to boiling in a medium-size saucepan. Meanwhile, in a bowl or measuring cup, gradually add ¾ cup of the cornmeal to the milk, stirring briskly to make a smooth paste. Add the mixture to the boiling water, continuing to stir constantly. Cook for 4 or 5 minutes while adding the remaining cornmeal. When the mixture begins to pull away from the sides of the pot and stick together, remove from heat.

Dump bidia into a bowl. Then, with damp hands, shape it into a smooth ball, flipping it so that the rounded sides of the bowl help to smooth it. Serve immediately.

To eat in the traditional manner, tear off a small chunk and make an indentation in it with your thumb. Use this hollow as a "bowl" to scoop up sauces and stews.

Variations: For a less conventional, but delicious porridge, dump half a cup of yellow cornmeal into a cup or more of boiling water. It will form lumps, but if you stir and mash vigorously with a strong wire whisk, the lumps will disappear. Add more cornmeal as necessary until you have a consistency similar to cream of wheat. Cook for 3 or 4 minutes, stirring constantly. Serve hot.

Koushry
Rice and Lentils

Egypt

Serves 4-6

1 cup dark lentils, pre-soaked
1 cup long grain rice
1 tsp. salt
3 medium-size onions, finely
  chopped
2 tblsp. oil

Put lentils and rice in separate pots. Pour enough boiling water over lentils to cover them. Add 1½ cups boiling water to rice for white rice, or 2 cups if you're using brown rice. Simmer both rice and lentils, covered, over low heat for 15-20 minutes, drain, and combine in a large pot. Add salt and another half cup of water. Cover, and simmer another 15-20 minutes, or until rice and lentils are both tender. Add a bit more water if necessary to prevent burning.

Meanwhile, gently fry the onions in oil until they are golden brown. Stir them into the rice and lentils before serving.

Saffron Rice

Morocco

Serves 4-6 as a side dish

2 tblsp. butter or vegetable oil
1 medium-size yellow onion,
  chopped
1 green bell pepper, chopped
1 cup long grain rice
½ tsp. salt
¼ tsp. pepper
¼ tsp. saffron or turmeric

Heat oil in a large, heavy skillet or pot. Stir in butter, onion, pepper and rice. Fry over moderate heat, stirring frequently, until rice becomes golden, about 15 minutes. Add spices and 2 cups water, and bring to a boil. Then reduce heat, cover, and simmer about 20 minutes until liquid is absorbed.

Geel Rys   South Africa
Yellow Rice

Serves 4-6

4 tblsp. butter
2 cups long grain white rice
2 sticks cinnamon
1 tsp. salt
1 tsp. turmeric
1 cup raisins

Melt butter over moderate heat in a heavy, medium-size pot. Add rice, and stir until each grain is well coated. Then add cinnamon, salt and turmeric plus 2 cups of water. Bring to a boil, cover, and reduce heat to simmer. Cook for 20-30 minutes until water is absorbed and rice is tender.

Stir in the raisins and heat for another minute or so before serving.

Samp   Zambia
Pounded Corn

In parts of central and southern Africa, corn is left on the stalk to dry out before being harvested. The resulting hard kernels are pounded in a mortar and pestle. After being soaked and cooked, rather like dried legumes, they are eaten with other foods. The classic—and highly nutritious—combination is *samp and beans*. You can make your own approximation of it with canned hominy and an equal part of dried beans. Cook the beans, heat the hominy, and serve together. A cup of each will do for 6-8 people.

If you're determined to have the real thing, find field corn that has been dried on the stalk. Pop the brittle kernels off the cobs with your fingers and pound or grind them to loosen the tough husks. Put in a pot of cold water and skim off the husks that rise to the top. Soak for 2 days, drain, then spread one layer deep on a clean surface to dry in the sun. Store in a cool, dry place.

To cook, put the kernels in enough water to cover and simmer for 2-3 hours, until tender.

Salads

Fresh, raw vegetables are perfect accompaniments to nearly every food in this book. But even though you can't improve on a classic, simple green salad, these half-dozen recipes do offer delicious variety.

Eggplant Salad   Morocco

Serves 6

1 lb. eggplant, peeled and cubed
1 lb. tomatoes, chopped
2 tsp. paprika
1 tsp. salt
1 clove garlic, minced
Tabasco sauce to taste
4 tblsp. olive oil

In a saucepan, cover eggplant with cold water, bring to a boil, and cook for half an hour. Drain, and press with a spoon to remove excess moisture.

Combine eggplant and tomatoes with remaining ingredients. Sauté in moderately hot olive oil for about 5 minutes, stirring and mashing ingredients together. Chill before serving.

Eggplant and Peanut Salad   Sudan

Serves 4-6

2 medium-size eggplants, peeled
   and chopped
½ tsp. salt
3-4 tblsp. olive oil
juice of 1 lemon
¼ cup peanuts, coarsely ground
1 clove garlic, minced and
   crushed
½ tsp. pepper

Sprinkle the eggplant with salt and let sit for 10 minutes. Then, with your fingers or a fork, gently squeeze out the excess moisture.

In a heavy skillet, fry the pieces in hot oil until golden brown. Eggplant will become greasy if oil is too cool, but watch it carefully and stir often to prevent burning and sticking. Drain and chill.

Combine remaining ingredients and stir into the eggplant. Serve cold.

Rooibeet Slaai   South Africa
Red Beet Salad

Serves 4-6

4 medium-size beets, cooked
   and diced
1 small onion, finely chopped
½ tsp. sugar
½ tsp. salt
1-2 tblsp. vinegar

Combine beets and onions. Dissolve sugar and salt in vinegar. Pour over beets and mix well. Serve cold.

Raita   South Africa
Cucumber and Yogurt Salad

Serves 4-6

2 large cucumbers, grated or
   sliced in rounds
an amount of yogurt equal to
   cucumbers (1 cup to 1 cup,
   etc.)
½-1 tsp. cumin seeds
½-1 tsp. fresh mint, finely
   chopped (optional)

Mix cucumbers and yogurt. In a hot, cast-iron skillet, toast cumin seeds without oil until brown. Stir briskly to prevent burning. Pound the toasted seeds in a mortar and pestle and stir into the cucumbers and yogurt along with the mint. Serve cold as an accompaniment to curries.

140

Chlada Felfel   Algeria
Tomato and Green Pepper Salad

Serves 4

2 large green bell peppers
2 large ripe tomatoes, peeled
    (see *About peeling* in the Intro-
    duction) and thinly sliced
4 tblsp. olive oil
½ tblsp. wine vinegar
2 cloves garlic, minced and
    crushed
½ tsp. salt
¼ tsp. pepper
handful of black olives
handful of green olives
several anchovies (optional)

Broil the green peppers in an oven for several minutes, turning them 3 or 4 times, until the skin blisters. When they're cool enough to handle, peel, seed and chop them. Pile in the center of a serving plate, and arrange tomato slices around them.

Prepare a vinaigrette by mixing olive oil, vinegar, garlic, salt and pepper. Pour over the vegetables. Decorate with olives and anchovies.

Chickpea Salad   Morocco

Serves 6

1 cup dried chickpeas,
    pre-soaked
3 tblsp. olive oil
1½ tsp. lemon juice
½ tsp. salt
4 tblsp. parsley, finely chopped

Boil the chickpeas in water to cover until they are very tender, an hour or more. (You should be able to mash a cooked pea against the roof of your mouth with your tongue—but be care-ful to cool a pea before testing it!) Drain.

Combine the remaining ingredients and stir gently, but thoroughly, into the chickpeas. Chill until ready to serve.

Desserts

Although sweet snacks and candies are popular treats in many parts of Africa, desserts as such are not common except in South Africa and Zimbabwe, influenced by early European settlers, and Liberia, where freed slaves returning to Africa brought back a fondness for sugary baked goods. In general, the best way to end an African meal is with plain fresh fruit. For special occasions, though, try some of these special recipes.

Chlada Fakya   Algeria
Fruit Salad

Serves 6. Look for orange water at a specialty food store.

¼ of a melon, such as cantelope or honeydew, chopped into small pieces
2 apples, chopped into small pieces
2 bananas, sliced in rounds
5 oranges, peeled, chopped and seeded
juice of 2 oranges
juice of 2 lemons
2 tblsp. sugar
1 tblsp. orange water(optional)
1 tsp. vanilla
½ tsp. cinnamon

Combine all the fruit in a serving bowl. Sprinkle over it the juices, sugar, orange water, vanilla and cinnamon. Mix gently and chill before serving.

Orange Dessert Salad   Morocco

Serves 6

6 oranges, sliced in rounds and seeded
6 large pitted dates, chopped
6 sautéed almonds (see recipe, page 28), slivered
juice of ½ a lemon
1 tsp. cinnamon

Combine oranges, dates and almonds in a serving bowl. Gently stir in lemon juice and chill until ready to eat. Just before serving, sprinkle on the cinnamon.

143

Banana Fritters   Africa

Fruits or vegetables fried in deep fat are popular all over the African continent, as they traditionally have been in the southern United States (see About frying *in the Introduction). This recipe makes about 20 fritters.*

1½ cups flour
3 tblsp. sugar (optional)
¼ tsp. ground ginger
½ tsp. ground cinnamon
2-3 eggs
1 cup milk
5-6 medium-size bananas, well
  mashed
oil for deep frying
confectioners' sugar (optional)

In a large mixing bowl, combine flour, sugar, ginger and cinnamon. Beat in the eggs, one at a time, using a sturdy wire whisk. Gradually add the milk, continuing to beat until batter is smooth and satiny, about 5 minutes. Stir in the bananas and let the mixture sit for 10-15 minutes while oil is heating.

When oil is 350-375°, dip out about a quarter cup of the batter and pour it, all at once, quickly, into the hot oil. Let brown 2-3 minutes, then turn with a slotted spoon. If you are not expert at this process, your oil will fluctuate in temperature, so watch carefully and remove fritters when they are a rich, golden brown. Lay on clean, absorbent cloths to drain.

Continue until all batter is used. (As you gain confidence, you will be able to fry 3 or 4 fritters at a time.) If you want to save some of the batter for later use, cover bowl tightly and refrigerate. The batter will turn a streaky brown, but will be good for 2 or 3 days.) Keep the first-cooked fritters warm in a low oven while you fry more, but eat them as soon as possible. If you like, sprinkle with confectioners' sugar just before serving.

Cocada Amarela   Angola
Coconut Pudding

Serves 4-6. Our tests of this unusual dessert did not produce uniform results; perhaps skill at candy making would be helpful. But, however inconsistent the texture and appearance, the taste always seems to be wonderful. Sometimes a dozen eggs are used for one batch; this version is a little more modest.

1-1¼ cups sugar
6 whole cloves
meat from 1 fresh coconut,
    grated or ground in a blender
    or food processor (see page 6)
6 egg yolks
⅛ tsp. ground cinnamon
2 egg whites (optional)
1 tblsp. orange water (optional)

Combine 1 cup of the sugar, cloves, and about a cup of water in a large, heavy saucepan. Boil 7 or 8 minutes until mixture reaches a temperature of 230°, or until a small spoonful dropped into cold water forms coarse threads. With a slotted spoon, remove and discard the cloves.

Reduce heat to low and gradually stir in the coconut. Simmer 10-12 minutes until coconut becomes translucent, then remove pot from heat. In a large, heat-proof bowl, beat the egg yolks with cinnamon until they thicken slightly. Then gradually add the coconut mixture to the bowl, stirring constantly. When well mixed, scrape the contents of the bowl into the saucepan and return to the burner. Cook and stir over medium heat until mixture thickens, about 12-15 minutes. Spoon into individual custard cups and set aside.

To make a meringue topping, beat the egg whites until soft peaks form. Gradually add remaining sugar and beat until peaks are stiff, but not dry. Spoon meringue over each cup of hot pudding and bake in a 350° oven for a few minutes, until top is lightly browned.

If you prefer, put the pudding into a single serving dish. Eat warm or chilled.

Plantain Gingerbread   Liberia

Makes 1 9-inch square panful

⅓ cup butter
½ cup sugar
1 tsp. vanilla
2 large plantains, sliced in rounds
2⅓ cups flour
½ tsp. salt
1½ tsp. baking soda
2 tsp. ground ginger
1 tsp. ground cinnamon
½ tsp. ground cloves
1 cup dark molasses
1 cup milk

Use a tablespoon of the butter to grease a 9-inch square baking dish. Pre-heat oven to 350°.

Combine sugar and vanilla in a heavy saucepan with half a cup of water. Add plantain slices and cook over moderate heat until plantains are tender. Drain. Then layer slices across the bottom of the baking dish. Set aside.

Combine flour, salt, baking soda and spices in a bowl. In a clean saucepan, bring butter and molasses just to a boil. Begin adding the flour/spice mixture and the milk a bit at a time, alternating them. Beat vigorously. When all the remaining ingredients have been added to the pan, and mixture is smooth, pour over plantains in the baking dish. Bake 50 minutes to an hour, or until a knife inserted into the center comes out clean.

Chinchin

Nigeria

Fried Pastries

Makes about 3 dozen

1 cup butter
¾-1 cup sugar (depending on your taste)
4 eggs, beaten
3½-4 cups flour, sifted
½ tsp. baking powder
½ tsp. nutmeg
1 tblsp. grated orange rind
pinch of salt
peanut oil for deep frying

In a large mixing bowl, cream the butter and sugar by beating vigorously with a sturdy spoon or a large fork until mixture is light and creamy. (Butter should be near room temperature before you begin.) Add eggs one at a time, beating well after each is put in.

In a separate bowl, sift flour with baking powder, salt and nutmeg, and stir in orange rind. Gradually add flour mixture to the first bowl, beating all the while. Use just enough flour to make a stiff dough that pulls away from the side of the bowl and isn't too sticky. Turn out onto a lightly-floured surface and knead for 5 or 10 minutes until smooth. (Knead by pushing heels of hands down into the dough ball, then folding in the sides to re-form the ball. Repeat.)

Roll the dough out to a thickness of about ¼ inch, and cut into rectangular strips about 5 inches long and 2 inches wide. Cut a 2-inch long slit in the center of one half of each strip, and pull the other end part way through to form a loop. Then fry, 2 or 3 at a time, in deep fat, until golden brown. (See *About frying* in the Introduction.) Lay on clean, absorbent cloths to drain. Serve hot.

Mescouta
Date Cake

Makes 1 8-inch round cake

¾ cup butter
¾ cup flour
6 eggs
¼-½ cup sugar (depending on
  your liking for sweets)
1 tsp. vanilla
½ tsp. baking powder
1 cup pitted dates, chopped
½ cup walnuts, chopped
⅓ cup raisins

Morocco

Use 1 tablespoon of the flour to grease an 8-inch tube cake pan. Dust with a tablespoon of the flour. Set aside. Pre-heat oven to 325°.

Beat together the eggs, sugar, vanilla and baking powder. Melt remainder of the butter and add it, mixing well. Gradually stir in the flour, beating with a wooden spoon until well blended. Add dates, raisins and walnuts and stir again to distribute them evenly through the batter. Pour mixture into the prepared pan and bake about 30 minutes, until a knife inserted into the center comes out clean.

Mango Snow

Serves 6

4 unripe mangos, peeled and
  thinly-sliced
2 tblsp. sugar, or to taste

Tanzania

In a pot with just enough water to cover the bottom, steam the mango slices until they are very soft. Keep a close watch to make sure water doesn't simmer away, leaving mangos to burn or stick. Purée the cooked mangos in a blender or food processor along with the sugar, or mash mangos and sugar together until all lumps are gone. Serve immediately, or chill.

Variation: Whip 1 cup of heavy cream and fold it into chilled mango purée before serving.

148

Banana Enrolada
Banana Rolled in Pastry

Serves 4

Cape Verde

1½ cups flour
2 tblsp. sugar
½ tsp. salt
6 tblsp. butter, softened
4 very ripe bananas
oil for frying
cinnamon

Combine flour, sugar and salt in a mixing bowl. With your fingertips, work the butter into the flour mixture until it is well-distributed. Add water, a tablespoonful at a time, until you have a dough that will hold together in a ball. (If you have time, cover the pastry and refrigerate it for 30 minutes at this point.)

Turn the ball out onto a lightly floured surface and divide it into 4 parts. Roll each part into an oblong that is an inch or so longer than your bananas, and wide enough to wrap around one. Lay a banana on each oblong, and roll it up in the pastry, sealing the edges and ends by pinching with your fingertips.

Deep fry the pastry-wrapped bananas (see *About frying* in the Introduction), or fry them in an inch or so of hot oil in a large, heavy skillet for 3 or 4 minutes on each side. When done, they should be crisp and golden brown outside, and soft and moist inside. Drain on clean, absorbent cloths, and sprinkle with cinnamon before serving.

Melktert
Milk Tart

South Africa

Makes 2 9-inch pies. Milk tarts are regarded as the quintessential Afrikaans dessert. No church social is complete without one. A proper milk tart should be made with puff pastry— the preparation of which is a procedure beyond the scope of this cookbook. We've substituted a good basic pie dough.

For the crust:

2 cups flour
1 tsp. salt
⅔ cup butter or shortening

Pre-heat oven to 450°.

Begin with chilled ingredients and utensils, if possible (you can stick the mixing bowl and measuring implements in the freezer for a few minutes). Sift flour and salt together. If your're using butter, quickly grate it. Then rapidly work butter or shortening into the flour with your fingertips until you have a coarse, crumbly mixture.

Add 4 tablespoons of water and mix it in with a fork. Then try to shape the dough into a ball with your hands. If it won't hold together, add more water, a spoonful at a time until it will. But work quickly so that ingredients stay cold. When you have a ball that will stay together, roll it out into two circles that will fit in the bottoms of the pie plates and crinkle up the sides. Carefully transfer the pastry to the pie plates. Pierce crusts with a fork in several places to allow air to escape, but don't go all the way through. Bake for 6-8 minutes or until barely golden.

For the filling:

4 cups milk
1 cup sugar
2 tblsp. butter
2 cinnamon sticks
2 tblsp. flour
3 tblsp. corn starch
½ tsp. salt
4 eggs, separated into yolks and
  whites
½ tsp. vanilla
½ tsp. almond extract
½ tsp. ground cinnamon

Pre-heat oven to 400°.

In a heavy saucepan, bring just to a boil the milk, ⅓ cup of the sugar, and the butter and cinnamon sticks. Remove from heat.

Combine, in a separate bowl, the flour, corn starch, salt and another ⅓ cup of the sugar. Dip out about ¼ cup of the hot milk mixture and gradually stir it into the bowl, mixing well to prevent lumping. When you have a smooth paste, add the egg yolks and mix again. Slowly add this paste to the saucepan and return it to the heat. Cook at a moderate temperature, stirring constantly, until mixture thickens, about 5 minutes. Stir in vanilla and almond extract and remove from heat. Let cool for about 5 minutes.

Meanwhile, beat together the egg whites and the last of the sugar until the mixture is stiff but not dry. Fold this gently into the filling. Pour into the pie shells and bake for 10 minutes. Reduce oven temperature to 350° and bake for another 10-15 minutes. Serve hot.

Beverages

Water is the primary drink all over Africa, and even that is in short supply in this drought-plagued era. Sources of clean water, especially, are difficult to find.

To supplement water, most countries and regions have their own, time-tested ways of turning local plants into slightly fermented, often nutritious beverages, like Lesotho's *leting* and South Africa's *amarehwu*. Variations of fruit ciders, palm wines and honey beers are common everywhere. In some areas, milk is an important drink, although in other places it is consumed only by children, if available at all.

Perhaps the drink that makes the most impression on travelers is northern Africa's sugary mint tea, served with elaborate ceremony every day, several times a day. In this chapter, you can learn how to make your own tea, plus other north and west African favorites.

Yansoon   Egypt
Aniseed Drink

For each cup:

¾ cup water
1 tsp. aniseeds
2 tsp. sugar

Boil ingredients together for 2 minutes. Pour through a tea strainer into serving cups.

Lemon Grass Drink   West Africa

Grow lemon grass in your herb garden or on a sunny window sill and have your own supply for this west African refresher.

1 lb. lemon grass
½ gallon water
sugar to taste

Wash the lemon grass and put it in a large pot. Boil water, add it to grass, and cover. Brew for several minutes before adding sugar. Serve hot.

Khchaf   Algeria
Fruit Drink

2 quarts water
2 sticks cinnamon
½ cup raisins
1 tblsp. sugar (or sugar to taste)

Bring water with cinnamon sticks to a boil. Add raisins, reduce heat to low, and simmer for 15 minutes. Stir in sugar and let it melt. Then remove the pot from the heat and take out the cinnamon sticks. When liquid is completely cool, refrigerate it for about half an hour. Serve with or without raisins.

Almond Milk   Morocco

½ cup almonds
½ cup sugar
¾ cup water
4¼ cups milk
⅛ cup orange water, or 1 tblsp. orange rind, grated

It's easiest to make this drink in a blender or food processor. Grind almonds and half the sugar to a paste. Add half the water and let the mixture sit for a few minutes. Then grind again, gradually adding the remaining water. Let sit for 30 minutes.

Meanwhile, dissolve the rest of the sugar in the milk by stirring vigorously. Add the orange water. Then strain the almond liquid through a clean cloth or a fiber tea strainer. Stir into the milk. Serve immediately.

Ginger Beer   Africa

Home-made soft drinks brewed from fresh ginger can be found all across sub-Saharan Africa. They are made at varying ratios of water to ginger, and fruits of many varieties, such as pineapples and guavas, may be substituted for the citrus. This recipe produces a strong concentrate that can be diluted with equal parts water for drinking, but many people like it just as it is, over ice.

16 ounces (or a couple of large
   handfuls) fresh ginger
juice of 1 or 2 limes
1 stick cinnamon (optional)
1 tsp. whole cloves (optional)
1 cup sugar, or to taste

Wash the ginger and peel it, being careful to remove only the outer layer of skin. Grind or pound to a pulp, and place in a large, heat-proof container that is enameled or made of glass or stainless steel. Cover with ½ gallon (8 cups) of boiling water. Set the mixture aside in a warm place. (You may want to protect it from dust by covering the container loosely with a cloth.)

After an hour or so, strain the liquid through a cloth, squeezing pulp to extract all the flavor. Stir in lime juice, cinnamon, half the cloves and ½ gallon of cold water. Let liquid sit for another hour, in the sun if possible. (Rebecca Dyasi in the book *Good Tastes in Africa* says this is done to allow the starch from the ginger to settle.)

Pour the mixture gently through a cloth to strain it, trying not to disturb any sediment at the bottom. Strain again if necessary. Stir in the remaining cloves, then transfer the ginger beer to a jar and refrigerate.

Le Thé   Western Sahara
Mint/Tea

All across the arid territory that stretches in a swath down north-west Africa, the harshness of desert life is punctuated by the gentle ritual of the tea ceremony. Three or four times a day, work or travel—or war—comes to a halt while the drink is being prepared. Saharans use what they call *gunpowder* tea, a green leaf that they combine with chunks of sugar chipped off a large cone.

The tea is brewed in small brass pots, and drunk in 3-inch tall glasses that also are used as measures. To make 3 servings, fill half a small container, such as a liqueur glass, with green tea leaves. Put them in a warm pot. Add 2 glasses of boiling water. Shake pot for a moment, then pour the water away. This is the washing of the tea.

Now add several sprigs of fresh mint to the pot, along with up to 14 spoons of sugar. Pour in 3 glassfuls of boiling water. Let steam for a moment, then pour from the pot into a glass. Return liquid to the pot. Repeat the process of pouring tea back and forth between the pot and the glass several times. Taste (to decide whether to add more sugar!), then serve.

Repeat this entire process twice more, adding additional water and sugar to the pot, but not more tea. At the end, everyone will have had 3 glasses, each milder than the one before.

Saharans say that the first tea is bitter, like life; the second is sweet, like love; and the third is gentle, like death.

Index

Errata

Biryani, p. 58:
—6 small potatoes, peeled (in basic ingredients list) should read:
6 small potatoes, *boiled unpeeled* until tender but not mushy.

—When combining the various biryani ingredients for final cooking, you may either use the pre-cooked chicken pieces whole, or remove the meat from the bones before adding it to the pot.

Sales of **The Africa News Cookbook:** help support the work of

Africa News Service, a non-profit, educational news agency that provides information about Africa through
- a bi-weekly publication
- a satellite-distributed broadcast service
- a research and information service
- a library that is open to the public

If you are interested in subscribing to our publication or in getting your local public or commercial radio station to air our programs—or in offering advice, criticism or recipes for subsequent editions of the cookbook—contact us at
Box 3851, Durham, North Carolina 27702 (919) 286-0747

The Africa News Cookbook:
African Cooking for Western Kitchens
To order additional copies, clip out and return these order blanks.

- -

Return this form with a check to:
**Africa News Service   P.O. Box 3851
Durham, NC 27702**   tel: 919-286-0747

Choose conventional "perfect" binding (like most of the soft-covers in your bookstore) or —while they last —the lay-flat spiral binding that is increasingly popular for cookbooks.

NAME _____

ADDRESS _____

CITY _____ STATE _____ ZIP _____

TEL. _____

No. of Copies x	Price Per Copy =	Total
	$11.95 (perfect-bound)	
	$12.70 (spiral-bound)	
	Subtotal	
	Shipping & Handling (first copy)	$2.50*
	Plus $1.50 for each additional book	
	Amount Enclosed	

- -

Return this form with a check to:
**Africa News Service   P.O. Box 3851
Durham, NC 27702**   tel: 919-286-0747

Choose conventional "perfect" binding (like most of the soft-covers in your bookstore) or —while they last —the lay-flat spiral binding that is increasingly popular for cookbooks.

NAME _____

ADDRESS _____

CITY _____ STATE _____ ZIP _____

TEL. _____

No. of Copies x	Price Per Copy =	Total
	$11.95 (perfect-bound)	
	$12.70 (spiral-bound)	
	Subtotal	
	Shipping & Handling (first copy)	$2.50*
	Plus $1.50 for each additional book	
	Amount Enclosed	

*IMPORTANT: Shipping (via UPS) for amounts specified above includes only locations in the United States and Ontario, Canada. For shipment elsewhere, inquire about cost.